LESLIE LINSLEY

First Steps
In Stenciling

LESLIE LINSLEY

First Steps
In Stenciling

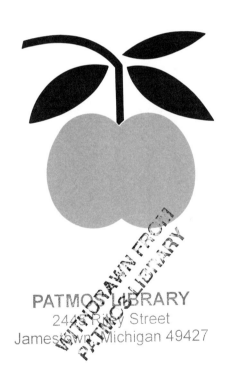

Photographs by Jon Aron

Illustrations by Peter Peluso, Jr.

Doubleday & Company, Inc., Garden City, New York

1986

Gift 8-10-03

Library of Congress Cataloging-in-Publication Data

Linsley, Leslie.
  First steps in stenciling.

  1. Stencil work.   I. Title.
TT270.L56 1986   745.7'3   86–2108
ISBN 0-385-19879-5
    0-385-23801-0 (pbk)

CONTENTS

Book Three

FIRST STEPS IN STENCILING ON FURNITURE   *1*

INTRODUCTION

Since this is to be first steps in stenciling, I will assume that you are a beginner and have never stenciled before. However, stenciling is such an easy craft to learn that once you've cut your first stencil and applied the paint to your object you will be on your way to professional status as a stenciler.

It's just a matter of becoming familiar with the materials and what you can do with them. You'll be surprised at how easy it is to take a simple design and create borders, overall patterns, and very elaborate scenes. You'll be able to use designs from wallpaper, fabric, and chinaware to adapt for decorative accessories and furnishings. In this way you can integrate your decorating. Stenciling is also an inexpensive way to add color and interest to small gift items, Christmas ornaments, notepaper, and clothing.

Stenciling involves the art of cutting a pattern into paper and applying color to the surface of an object through the cutout areas. When the cutout template is removed, the pattern is discernible. The design is accurately positioned with clean, sharp, well-defined edges. Once a stencil design is cut you can use it over and over, varying the placement and arrangement so each appears differently.

A technique used extensively in America in the eighteenth and nineteenth centuries, stenciling is now enjoying a revival with modern craftworkers. New and improved tools and materials have made it easy to recreate Early American motifs often found on furniture and walls in old New England homes as well as to create original designs. Perhaps the most familiar old designs are the stenciled motifs found on Boston rockers and Hitchcock chairs. Another popular stenciled item copied from Early American days is the canvas or oilcloth floor covering. These were often stenciled with elaborate scenes and borders, the effect intended to be that of an expensive carpet or floor painting. The modern version of this item is taken from a quilt appliqué, such as the popular schoolhouse design, stenciled on canvas.

In Europe during the early part of the nineteenth century, expensive-looking "wallpaper" was actually a repeated stencil design. Early stencilers painted swags and tassels to imitate gathered drapery, columns, elegant urns as well as flowers, pinecones, leaves, and fruit. The pineapple was a very popular design, representing hospitality. Today this is still the most widely used design on furniture, fabric, and walls.

There are many precut commercial stencils on the market; however, these designs are limited and certainly not customized for your particular needs.

The best thing about the craft of stenciling is that anyone can achieve perfect results. Imagine being about to create a perfect design on any surface . . . over and over again. A simple design is good for starters and there are many ways to create a look that is professional and exquisite without being difficult. No special talent is required. The tools and materials are basic and inexpensive and the design potential is limitless.

Each of the projects in this book is designed so that you can do it quickly and easily. In this way you will achieve immediate results, thus enabling you to go on with the craft. All the technical information is provided in the following section so that you can refer to it as needed. At the end of this section you will find a source list of mail order suppliers. Each carries a variety of precut stencil designs as well as papers and brushes that will help you do the craft. Some carry a line of paints in country colors for wood and fabric items. You will also find a wide variety of letters and numbers in different typefaces and sizes in most hardware, art, and stationery stores. These are excellent for making signs, personalizing gift items such as luggage tags, and for making plaques with sayings or verse.

So, look over the materials you will need, find a project that is just right for you, and we'll get started with your first steps in stenciling.

General stenciling materials

All the materials you need are readily available and inexpensive. Therefore, I recommend buying a good set of brushes, paints, and papers, since these are all that is necessary to get you started. If you have a good art supply store in your area, buy your materials there. If you start with the proper tools, it will be easier to create perfect stencils.

Stencils

There are precut stencils sold as kits, but each project presented here has an original design for you to trace and cut out. You can then use these stencils on a variety of projects of different sizes.

To cut a stencil design you will need stencil paper. This is a wax-coated, slightly stiff paper that prevents the design from slipping while you work with it on a surface. It is excellent for large projects such as walls. Acetate or vinyl are preferred by many stencilers because they will give you clean, sharp edges, last longer than paper, can be sponged clean, and will stick to a surface. You can buy it in rolls by the yard or use the sleeves from photo albums. It is fairly inexpensive.

Oaktag (tagboard), manila folders, and Mylar are other materials for cutting a stencil. Both the oaktag and folder are fine for a one-time use on a small object, but they get wet and frayed after having paint tapped over them many times. Mylar is as good as acetate but may be harder to find.

I prefer the waxed paper because it's easy to cut, lasts long enough to finish any project, and is relatively inexpensive. Though I've often found it in a variety of stores, it may be difficult to find in some areas. If so, I recommend vinyl or acetate.

Cutting tools

For cutting out a stencil you will need a craft knife with a narrow handle that is easy to hold, like a pencil. An X-acto craft knife with a #11 blade is best. Buy an extra package of blades with the knife.

Brushes

Stencil brushes are called stipple brushes and come in various sizes. For the following projects you will need two or three brushes in a small and a medium size. The better the brush the better the results. This is an area where saving money is not always practical, but the best brushes are not always the most expensive. Your art store dealer will be able to advise you.

You will need a different brush for each color. Only buy brushes with natural bristles. Regular paintbrushes are an absolute no-no. You need the real thing.

Paint

Acrylic paint is the only kind that is practical to use for stenciling. Even the stencil purists agree that acrylic paint is the best, for the following reasons: You can buy it in small tubes and in every color imaginable; it washes off hands and brushes and is permanent on all surfaces; it is especially ideal for fabric stenciling, since a stenciled piece of clothing, tablecloth, or curtains can be washed and the stencil will not wash away.

The brands of paint most readily available in art stores and five-and-dimes are Liquitex and Grumbacher. Always buy a tube of white to mix with the colors, as even the pastels are usually too bright; a drop of color goes a long way. To lighten a color you will add white, and to darken a color you will add black or brown.

Latex has the same good qualities and can be used right from the can. Most paint manufacturers have developed Colonial colors and this is an added advantage to the stenciler who wants to recreate an authentic Early American design. Always ask for a flat finish rather than a semi- or high-gloss latex. A pint of paint is plenty for almost any project.

Tracing paper

Most of the designs in this book are shown full size. However, if you are copying a design or need to enlarge one here you will need tracing paper, a pencil, and grid paper (see next section for how to enlarge a design).

Helpful items

A *small saucer* is ideal for mixing paint colors. Since you are using water-base paint it is easy to clean the dishes with warm water. *Paper plates* are also good for this. Be sure to have one for each color.

Masking tape is used to hold your stencil in place over the surface. Buy the three-quarter to one-inch width.

A *straightedge* is especially important when creating borders. You will also need a *fine marker* to trace the design.

Remember to protect the table on which you will cut your stencil. The *cutting surface* should be heavy cardboard or a wooden board.

You will also need a *small sponge* or *dry cloth* to wipe away any slight errors. An *artist's brush* with a small narrow point is indispensable for touching up, adding a dot of color in the center of a flower, or adding details such as veins on leaves. An artist's *palette knife* is useful for mixing acrylic paint colors.

Sources of stenciling materials

Extra Special Products Inc.
P.O. Box 777
Greenville, OH 45331
Waxed stencil paper in mini sizes seems to be their specialty. These are good for small projects.

Illinois Bronze Paint Co.
300 E. Main St.
Lake Zurich, IL 60047
This company carries a line of country colors in acrylic and fabric paints. They also have separate kits of stencil designs with precut stencils. They are available in paint stores and hobby shops.

Stencil Craft
160 Emerald St.
Keene, NH 03431

Stencil-Ease
P.O. Box 209
New Ipswich, NH 03071
This is a wholesaler carrying an extensive line of stencil products. Write to them for a source of supplies in your area.

Whole Kit & Kaboodle Co.
8 West 19th St.
New York, NY 10011
(catalog $1.50)
This company has an extensive line of products and the catalog is well worth ordering. Their stencil brushes are especially good.

You and Me Patterns, Inc.
Rt. 1, Box 170
Owatonna, MN 55060
Their specialty is Teddy Bears for which they have precut stencils 2 inches high.

Art supplies

Arthur Brown, Inc.
2 West 46th St.
New York, NY 10036

Charrette
31 Olympia Ave.
Woburn, MA 01801
(catalog $1)

Boxes and wood products

Adventures in Crafts Studio
P.O. Box 6058
Yorkville Station
New York, NY 10028

The Cracker Barrel
527 Narberth Ave.
Haddonfield, NJ 08033
Mushroom baskets, good for stencils.

Houston Art and Frame Co.
P.O. Box 4716
Houston, TX 77027

Preparing to stencil

While each project in the book features step-by-step directions, there are some general tips and how-to's that pertain to all the projects or to stenciling in general. These can be most helpful, especially when working on your own designs or on several projects at once.

The following directions will tell you the best ways to do the various steps in stenciling. Refer back to them as needed.

Enlarging a design

Although most of the designs have been presented full-size, occasionally it is necessary to enlarge or reduce a design to fit your object. If you are copying a design from another source it may be necessary to change the size.

To enlarge a design: Trace it as it is, then use a ruler to mark horizontal and vertical lines over the design to create a grid, or you can trace the design onto 1/4-inch graph paper. Next, number each square down and across for easy reference when enlarging the design.

Rule off a piece of paper with a larger grid, or use graph paper with larger squares. Num-

Original design

ber the squares on your large grid to correspond to the squares on the smaller grid. Copy the design square by square on the new grid. For example, 1/2-inch graph paper will enlarge the design twice the size, 1-inch graph paper will give you a design four times the original size.

Reducing a design

When a design is too large for your object, you can reduce the design with the grid method used for enlarging.

Trace the design and draw a large grid, such as 1-inch, over the design. Number the squares across and down. Using a smaller grid or graph paper such as 1/4-inch, copy the design square by square to the appropriate size.

This method is especially good when you want to use a design found in your curtains or couch fabric, for example on a small box or lampshade.

Cutting a stencil

Tape your stencil paper to your traced design. You should be able to see the design through your stencil paper, vinyl or acetate material. Do not tape these to the cutting surface. You want to be able to move the paper around as you cut the stencil.

Hold the knife as if it were a pencil. Apply pressure and cut along the marked lines, pull-

Enlarged design

ing the blade toward you. Use long, smooth strokes and turn the stencil with your free hand as you cut. Avoid short, choppy cuts. Cut the small areas first to keep the stencil from weakening. When two lines meet at a corner, cut past them very slightly where they intersect. This will give you sharp angles. If you make an error or cut too far into a line, it can be taped on both sides of the stencil paper.

The reason for the plain white paper is to save the design. When you remove your cut stencil you will have a second stencil cut through the white paper. If you need to cut another stencil at another time, you can trace the design from this.

Bridges and ties

Sometimes a design is so fragile that it would fall apart by the time you finished cutting it. Or, if you're cutting stencil letters the solid area of a P or an O, for example, would fall out. In order to hold the elements together, narrow strips of the stencil paper are left uncut. These are called bridges or ties.

To create a round stencil, the center piece has to be kept intact. To do this you would cut the O in segments separated by 1/2-inch bridges that are not cut. These hold the stencil together and create part of the design.

Bridge

Two-color stencils

If two or more colors touch, it's a good idea to have a stencil for each color. For example, if you have a red flower with a green stem and leaves, you'll cut a flower stencil without the stem and leaves. Then you'll cut a stem-and-leaf stencil without the flower. When you stencil one color, you will have to make sure that it is properly placed in relation to the other on your object. This is achieved with register marks.

Register marks

Register marks are used to match up each element of the stencil design. For example, when cutting the second color stencil, cut out part of the elements from the first color stencil. After you stencil the first color, such as the petals of a flower, you will place the second stencil or stem and leaves in place on the object. Since you have cut out elements from

First stencil   *Second stencil*

the first stencil onto this new stencil, in this case part of the flower, use that portion to guide your placement of the new stencil. If the colors touch, remember to cover that part of the flower when stenciling the stem and leaves. Simply mask it out by taping a piece of paper over the "register" area. This is the way you ensure perfect placement of each element of the design. Your stencil will be in balance each time you repeat the design. Without the register marks, you would not know exactly where to place the design on the second stencil.

Creating a straight border

If you are stenciling a border design, use a strip of masking tape to create a straight line above which you will add the stencil. Once finished, you can remove the tape and the border will be as perfect as the placement of tape in relation to the background.

Border stencils

A repeat modular design is often used as decoration to create borders around the top of walls, around wainscoting, windows, and floors. They can be quite narrow or as wide as you want. They can be geometric, a continuous band interrupted regularly by another design such as a flower, or individual, repeated, spot designs that create a border effect. This might be a series of ducks or teddy bears evenly spaced around the wall of a child's room.

When doing a border design the stencil will need register marks so you can match up

Partial designs are cut as register marks

the continuing design. This requires cutting part of the design to the right and left of the central cutout. As you continue to stencil, place the design on your surface to the right or left of the previous application so that the register mark is over the matching stencil you have just completed. The second stencil is repeated, but do not stencil the cutout register marks on either side of it. This is the way you keep a continuous design in perfect balance and evenly spaced throughout the project.

Mixing paints

It takes some trial and error to mix colors accurately. It only takes a small amount of paint for most of these projects. A palette knife is useful for blending acrylic paint on a flat dish or small saucer. However, any flat utensil such as a butter knife, Popsicle stick, or putty knife can also be used for mixing. If you're mixing several colors use a paper plate for each.

To mix a pastel color, for example, use a flat mixing tool and a paper plate or saucer, squirt about 1 tablespoonful of white acrylic paint onto the plate. To this add the tiniest spot of color. Blend the paints until there are no streaks of white or color. I always keep several paper plates handy for mixing paints, as this process will be repeated many times before arriving at the desired color.

When mixing two colors to achieve a third, you might want to refer to a color wheel, available in art and paint stores. But again, it simply takes a lot of experimenting to reach the color you may be trying to match.

Once you've gotten the color, mix enough paint to finish the project. It's very difficult to remix and match a color, especially after it's dry. When stenciling a large item, place a wet paper towel over the dish of paint to keep it from drying out.

Stenciling

Right away I will warn you: The biggest mistake in stenciling is too much paint on your brush. If the brush is not dry enough the paint will seep under the stencil, causing the edges of your design to be fuzzy rather than crisp and sharp. The center of the stencil will be heavy with color, which is not desirable.

1. Position the stencil sheet on the object and tape it on each corner so it won't slip. Hold your brush in an upright position so that when you dip the end bristles into the paint it coats them evenly. Dip the brush into the paint and then tap it up and down on newspaper several times to remove all excess paint. The paint should go on almost dry. A dry brush will achieve a clean, sharp design. I can't emphasize this enough. This is most important for a successful stencil and yet the hardest thing for a beginner to understand. The paint on your brush should feel dry to the touch.

2. With the brush straight up and down tamp the paint onto the area to be stenciled. This tapping motion is called "stippling." If you use a hard pounce, the dry brush will cover the area and you will avoid smearing and bleeding under the stencil. It is that up-and-down pouncing that allows you to cover the area so that it becomes more dense as you continue to do this. The effect is almost that of a mottled finish. Do not add more paint to the brush even if the stencil looks like it needs more.

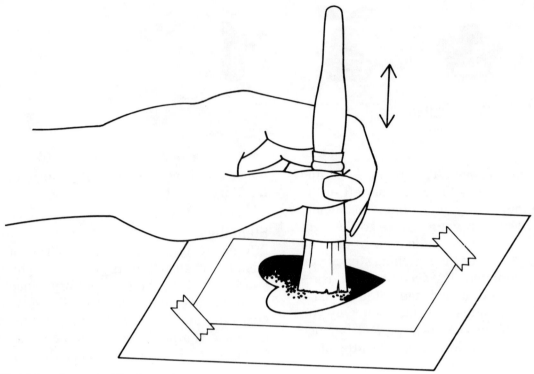

Hold brush perpendicular

3. Tap away from the edges so that excess paint doesn't get under the stencil. Let the paint dry on an area, then apply another coat if needed. When this is complete, carefully lift the stencil sheet to check the design. Always work on one section of the design at a time. Let each section dry before laying the stencil sheet over it to do the next section.

4. Apply one color to all appropriate areas before moving on to the next color. If you are using a 2-color stencil, it is best to apply the light color first, followed by the darker color. Save a little paint of each color for possible touch-ups. If you place a wet paper towel over the paint in your dish or cup, it will keep acrylic paint from drying out while you are working with another color.

5. Never let paint dry on the brush. Always clean your brush in warm water and be sure it is thoroughly dry before using it again. I often put my brushes on a radiator to dry. A hair dryer also speeds up the drying process. Be sure to clean the undersides of your stencils if paint gets on them.

6. For each succeeding color, place the appropriate stencil down with register marks in place. Using a new or clean brush for each color, continue to stencil as before. When you peel the stencil sheet away for the last time, you will be amazed. The design will be crisply executed and you will be inspired to do more.

Correcting mistakes

Wipe away any mistakes immediately while the paint is wet. A damp sponge will remove the paint. Small errors like rough edges aren't a problem. With stenciling, the eye adjusts to the overall design, not the little details that you see when working on a small area.

Fabric stenciling

Almost any fabric can be stenciled, which means the possibilities are extensive. For example, you can stencil curtains to match a wall or furniture stencil. You can stencil fabric to make pillows or upholstery, a tablecloth, napkins, wall hanging, even clothing.

As with stencil on a hard surface, acrylic paint is the easiest to work with for the best results. The only real difference is that mistakes cannot be corrected.

1. Wash the fabric, dry and iron before stenciling. Press while damp. This removes any sizing and, if the fabric shrinks, it will do so before you've stenciled it.
2. Pad your work surface with several layers of newspaper or a blotter. Any paint that goes through the fabric will then be absorbed. Tape the fabric so it is taut on the surface. When you move the fabric to stencil another area, place clean blotter paper under the fabric so excess paint won't come through from the underside.

3. Use the same stippling motion as for stenciling on a hard surface. Remember to tap off all excess paint from your brush to avoid any bleeding on the fabric. If the brush is too wet with paint, the design will be heavy and blurred. Again, a successful stenciling project is achieved with an almost-dry brush. This will also keep the fabric soft and pliable rather than stiff where the designs appear. As you approach the edge of the stencil, tap inward, away from the edge so that your color is evenly placed.
4. Apply the colors in the correct sequence for the design.
5. As on hard surfaces, acrylic paint dries on fabric almost immediately. Fabric paints can be set with a warm, dry iron. Place a dry cloth over the design and iron over it for 3 to 5 minutes. Acrylic paint doesn't need setting. It is now colorfast. Once applied to the fabric, it can be washed without fear of fading or running.

PLATE 1   Borders for Baby

PLATE 2   Country Corner

PLATE 3   *Blanket Chest, Spice Rack, Utensil Holder*

PLATE 4 *Country Pillows*

PLATE 5   Tile Trivet, All-Purpose Boxes, Kitchen Plaque, and Salt Box

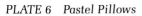

PLATE 6   Pastel Pillows

Book One

First Steps in Stenciling
Home Accessories

Within any style of decorating, whether it's country, colonial, traditional, or contemporary, we search for a way to express our own identity. Sometimes this personal stamp is created by adding a handcrafted item to the room. In this way we immediately create visual stimulation to produce dramatic results. It doesn't have to cost a great deal of money to do something tasteful. For example, the sheets and pillowcase project shown on the following pages demonstrates how you can change a plain, inexpensive purchased item into a unique, "one-of-a-kind" with a simple stencil design. This is probably one of the easiest projects to do in an afternoon.

Another example is the tablecloth with matching seat cushions for a kitchen corner. The pineapple design is inspired by the wallpaper in the room and the stencil is adapted for the specific size of the furniture. You can use any design from wallpaper, fabric, even your chinaware, for a stencil. In this way you can integrate the various objects in a room setting, adding color and contrast where needed.

It's these finishing touches that make a home personal. Handcrafting doesn't necessarily conform to decorating trends and this allows for freedom to express individuality and to lend character to a room.

Stenciling can be applied to a variety of background materials. The same design, paint and technique are used on fabric as well as wood. The desk, curtains, mirror frame and wall panel are decorated with the same border designs, which are changed only slightly to create interest and to fit the approximate areas to be stenciled. If you use one design on several different objects, changing the colors for each object will often give each item an entirely different look.

The country pillows demonstrate the use of Early American quilt designs in stenciling. Because these two crafts were prevalent at the same time in this country, we often see a crossover in designs for both techniques. This is another way to integrate designs in a room. One appliqué from a quilt block might be reduced for a stencil to fit on a jewelry box, or enlarged for a furniture stencil. (See pages x–xi for enlarging and reducing designs.)

BORDERS FOR BABY

For very little time, money, and expertise you can transform almost any purchased item into a unique and decorative baby accessory. Plain, colorful sheets are excellent for receiving a stencil design. Acrylic paint goes on evenly and permanently. Once dry it is completely washable without fading, bleeding, or disappearing. Be sure to use baby-safe paints. Check the labels.

There are a variety of designs that create a lively border. The duck, teddy bear, and other shapes presented here are easy beginner stencils to cut. Since they can be used to create a border design, you can use them around the room on the walls, across the bottom of a window shade, on a lampshade or on a crib. If used individually the design is adorable for a T-shirt, a diaper bag, the back of a rocking chair, or on other accessories in the room.

Materials

Colored single sheet and pillowcase (can be 100 percent or cotton blend); tracing paper; masking tape; pencil; plain white paper; X-acto craft knife; stencil paper (waxed or acetate); small- and medium-size stipple brushes; small tubes of acrylic paint in white, bright yellow or orange, and black (very small amount); saucers or paper plates.

Directions

For this first project we are sticking to the most basic stencil design because this is the best way to learn. If you want to add more designs to this border, you can do so later on.

Cutting the stencil

1. Begin with a tracing to use as a guide. To do this, first draw a straight line across the bottom of the tracing paper. Next trace the duck along this line two times, leaving a 2 1/2-inch space between them from the bill of one duck to the tail feathers of the other. If you are using one of the other designs, measure across the item and space each design element evenly across the object to be stenciled.

   When you are stenciling a border design it will be more accurate if the repeat pattern is cut from one stencil so that each element is spaced exactly the desired distance from the next. If you were to cut one stencil, you would have to measure and accurately position it on the sheet each time you placed it down. By cutting two ducks, for example, the spacing is incorporated into the design layout and serves as a register mark.

2. Tape your stencil paper onto your traced design. You will be able to see the design through the stencil paper or acetate. Do not tape to the surface. You

Duck motif for baby border

want to be able to turn the stencil as you cut.

3. Hold your craft knife in a comfortable position as with a pencil and, using smooth strokes, cut out the body of the duck, but not the feet and bill. Since this is a 2-color stencil where the colors touch, you will cut a separate stencil for each color.

4. Remove the cut stencil sheet and set aside. Tape another piece of stencil paper or acetate over the tracing and cut out the feet and bill in position as they will appear with the body. Remove this second stencil. You will now have a complete stencil cut from the white paper under all. Save this for later use to make a new stencil if needed.

Stenciling

1. Pad your table with paper or a blotter and tape the edge of the fabric sheet over this so it is taut. Decide where on the sheet the stenciled ducks will be placed. If the hem is quite wide, you might place them in this area. If your sheet has a narrow hem, the ducks will fit better along the top of the hemline.

2. Find the center of your hemline and tape the second stencil (the one with feet and bill only) in position so that the space between the ducks is over the center of the sheet and the feet are above the hemline.

Usually when there is a 2-color stencil, the lighter color is applied first. However, in this case you want to be sure that all feet are above the hemline.

3. Squirt a small amount of yellow or orange acrylic paint in a saucer or on a paper plate. Using the small brush, dip it into the paint. (When stippling, do not overload the brush with paint.) Hold the brush upright and tap up and down on newspaper to remove all excess paint. Your brush should be almost dry.

4. With one hand hold the stencil sheet down against the fabric. Tap up and down through the center of the cutout, filling the feet areas with color. Continue to do this, without adding more paint to your brush, until the entire area

5

is filled in. Repeat on the cutout area for the duck's bill.

5. Lift the stencil and reposition to the left or right of the first stencils. You have already applied the elements for 2 ducks. When you place the stencil down again, one of the cutouts should cover a previously painted stencil in order to position the new stencil. In other words, you did 2 stencils at once the first time. Now you will only stencil one duck at a time.

   Work back and forth on each side until you reach the edges of the sheet. In this way one stencil can be drying while you work on the other side.

   Be sure to check yourself so that the ducks are always lined up correctly. When finished with this color, rinse the brush in warm water and set aside to dry.

6. Next, tape the first stencil (duck body and head) in position between the feet and bill on the fabric. Be sure it is touching the feet and bill at the proper points.

7. Squirt a small amount of white paint on a saucer or paper plate and, using your medium-size brush (or thoroughly dry smaller brush), stencil the body as you did the feet and bills.

   If your background is a color, the white paint may not cover it completely on the first application. If color shows through, do *not* lift your stencil paper. Let the paint dry, then reapply, always using an almost-dry brush with a small amount of paint.

8. When you have finished all the designs across the fabric, place a small black dot of paint to create the eye on the duck's head. This can be done with a pointed artist's brush or the end of a pencil dipped in paint.

To finish

Let the paint dry for a few minutes. Acrylic paint dries almost instantly. Place the fabric face down on a dry cloth and set the color with a dry, medium-hot iron. This will remove any excess color from the sheet and make it colorfast for safe washing.

If you want to add an initial to personalize this project, you can stencil it in the center of the sheet between 2 ducks. Or, if you prefer, embroider a pretty letter with a contrasting or matching color thread.

Pillowcase

The pillowcase is done in the same way. Find the center of the front edge and work toward the outer edges. Be sure to place several pieces of paper or cardboard inside the pillowcase under the area you are stenciling. For a final touch, run a line of rickrack trim along the stitched hemline of the sheet and pillowcase.

Finally, the duck is only one motif you could use for a child's room. Other stencil ideas are included here—or, you could design one of your own.

Additional designs for baby borders

COUNTRY CORNER

Your wallpaper is a perfect potential design for furniture or, in this case, the tablecloth and seat cushions. Often a small design that interests you can be blown up to serve as decoration on a larger scale.

The pineapple design used here is a familiar, traditional Early American symbol representing hospitality. Many New England homes, especially in Maine, had a pineapple stencil adorning a table or the walls. This design is still one of the most popular used by modern-day stencilers.

Though I've used it on fabric, the same design can be applied to a painted surface. Perhaps you'd like to use it on a metal tray or directly on your table and chair seats.

Materials

Tracing paper; pencil; masking tape; stencil paper; X-acto knife; burnt orange, green, mustard, and blue acrylic paints; stipple brushes (2 or 3 medium-size); paper plates or saucers.

For tablecloth: muslin; hem facing in a color to match one of the paint colors; white eyelet trim.

For chair cushions: muslin; welting; Polyfil® stuffing.

Directions

Unbleached muslin is a good background material for stenciling. It receives acrylic paint well and sets off the paint colors of Early American designs. It comes in 45-, 52-, and 60-inch widths and sells for approximately $4.00 a yard.

To make the tablecloth
Measure across the top of your table. Next, measure from the tabletop edge down the side to the floor or to the length you desire. Double this last measurement and add the top measure for the amount of fabric needed.

For a floor-length tablecloth to fit a 42-inch round table (which is the most common size) you will need 6 yards of 45-inch-wide fabric.

Cut the fabric in half, which will give you two 3-yard pieces of muslin. Cut one of the 3-yard pieces in half lengthwise.

Sew each narrow piece to either side edge of the 45-inch-wide piece to create a seam at each side.

For all round tables
Find the center of the fabric. Attach a long string to the end of a pencil. Pin the end of the string to the center of the cloth (or have another person hold it there) and, with string taut, bring the pencil end to the edge of the fabric. Draw a wide circle by swinging the pencil around the fabric in a sweeping mo-

tion. Remove excess material by cutting along penciled circle line.

Position the fabric on your table and pin the eyelet so that it covers the raw edge of the fabric. Pin the hem facing over the top edge of the eyelet and stitch around.

To make the chair cushions

Using newspaper or brown wrapping paper, make a template the size and shape of your chair seats. If your seats are round or square, simply measure them and add 1/2 inch all around for seam allowance.

Cut 2 pieces of muslin for each cushion. Measure around each and cut the welting so it is 1/2 inch longer than the diameter of the cushion.

With raw edges aligned and welting toward the center of the cushion front, pin welting all around. Stitch welting to the fabric starting 1 inch from one end. Finish sewing with 1 inch overlapping at the end.

Do not stitch top and bottom cushion pieces together at this time.

Cutting the stencils

The pineapple and border designs appear full size and will fit almost any tabletop.

1. Trace the designs from the book and place the tracing over your tablecloth on the table to see if you like the way it looks. If it appears too large or too small, you can enlarge or reduce the design accordingly. (See pages x–xi.)
2. Tape the stencil paper over the tracing-paper design. Place this on a padded cutting surface.
3. With a sharp blade in your craft knife, cut out each element of the pineapple design. Though this is a 2-color stencil, the colors don't touch; therefore you won't need two different stencils.
4. To make the border fit your table, draw part of the curve of your table on a piece of tracing paper. Trace the pattern pieces on this curve, alternating leaf shape, dot, leaf shape, etc. Use this trac-

ing to cut out your stencil. (See photograph.)

Stenciling

1. Mix each paint color in a separate dish.
2. Be sure to tape the fabric at each corner so it is taut on a well-padded table. Cover the areas not being stenciled, since the paint, if spattered, is not removable.

   Locate the center of the tablecloth and tape the pineapple stencil cutout in place with a small piece of masking tape at each corner of the stencil.
3. Place a piece of masking tape over the ends of the leaf areas where they meet the body of the pineapple to avoid accidentally stenciling this section.
4. Using an almost-dry brush, stipple the burnt orange color onto the fabric through the stencil. Let dry.
5. Carefully remove the masking tape from the leaf area and place it over the top of the body where you have just stenciled. Or you can place a piece of paper over this painted section.
6. With very little green paint on a new brush, stipple the leaves onto the fabric. Let dry and remove the stencil sheet.
7. Repeat this process on the center of each cushion top.

Border

Draw an inner circle on the fabric where the border will be placed. Beginning at the edge of the drawn circle above the pineapple, stencil the border with blue paint all the way around. To do this you will place the stencil on the fabric, apply the paint to a section, and remove the stencil. When repositioning it, place the stencil over the last element that was painted in order to continue the balance and proper spacing all the way around.

Clean the stencil sheet so there is no blue paint on the paper. Tape the stencil on the fabric so it is inside the first border and, using a clean brush, stencil with the mustard-color paint.

Pineapple stencil

Pineapple leaves and border stencils

Finish seat cushions

When the paint is dry, place the bottom piece of muslin over the stenciled top and pin all around, leaving a 4-inch opening. Stitch together with welting between.

Clip around seam allowance to stitch line and turn right side out. Fill loosely with Polyfil® stuffing. Stitch opening closed with a slip stitch.

If desired, add ribbon or hem-facing ties to the back of each cushion to attach to the chairs.

BLANKET CHEST

A stencil design is the perfect way to decorate and make an unfinished piece of furniture interesting.

A blanket chest is a fairly common item and is sold for toy storage as well. The square or rectangular shapes make it easy to apply borders around the top, front, and sides.

The flower design begins in the center and leans to the left, then is flopped and repeated in the opposite direction. The flowers that meet in the center are joined with overlapping stems. The design will fit any size object and can also be used across dresser drawers, for example. This is a 2-color design. Because the colors touch, two separate stencils are needed.

Materials

Wooden chest; fine and medium sandpaper; primer paint; latex paint in background color (light green used here); 2-inch-wide paintbrush (sponge brush is good and inexpensive, available in hardware stores); tracing paper; pencil; masking tape; white paper; stencil paper; X-acto knife; dark green, yellow, and small amount of brown acrylic paint; stencil brushes; saucers or paper plates; varnish (optional).

Directions

Most unfinished furniture pieces need a light sanding to smooth the grain before painting. With medium-grade paper, sand in the direction of the grain and wipe away sand dust.

Give the entire box a coat of primer paint and don't forget inside the rim. You can paint the inside as well if desired. Let dry and apply two coats of your background latex color. Lightly sand the dry, painted surface with the fine sandpaper.

Preparing the design

1. Tape several pieces of tracing paper together to cover the top of your furniture piece.
2. Find the center of the area to be stenciled and mark this lightly with a pencil. Mark the tracing paper as well.
3. Trace the flower design so that the center of the stem crosses the center mark and leans to the right or left. Turn the tracing paper over and retrace the flower leaning in the opposite direction. The marked line should appear where the two stems cross each other.
4. Continue to trace the flowers on either side of the center so they are evenly spaced. The bottom of each stem should be even along the bottom edge of the ob-

Blanket chest flower stencil

ject. If you end up with half a flower at either end, you will have to adjust the spacing before cutting a stencil. Save the tracing to use as a guide.

Cutting the stencil

1. Trace 2 flowers on a separate piece of paper. Tape the stencil paper over this and place on a cutting surface.

2. Using your X-acto knife, cut out the stem and leaves to make one stencil. Remove the stencil paper and set aside. Turn the second traced design over and cut another stencil in the same way.

3. Tape a small piece of stencil paper over the flower tracing and cut out the flower shape. Remove the stencil paper, turn the tracing over, and cut another flower. You now have 2 stencils leaning to the left and 2 leaning to the right.

Stenciling

1. Tape the top corners of the complete traced design to the top of your wooden object.
2. Squirt a small amount of green paint on a saucer or on a paper plate.
3. Slide the stem-and-leaf stencil under the tracing edge that has not been taped down, and line it up so it is in register with the overlay tracing of the center flower. Lift the tracing and tape the stencil in position.
4. Dip your brush into the paint. Tap it up and down on scrap paper to remove most of the paint and pounce over the cutout until all areas are filled with green paint.
5. Continue to do this, moving the stencil in register under your tracing guide. Repeat in the opposite direction with your second matching stencil.
6. Next slide the flower stencil under the tracing, get it into register, and tape it in position.
7. Use a small amount of yellow paint and stencil the flower heads with a clean brush. Save this paint for your border.
8. Remove the flower stencils and cut a hole in the center of each. Hold each stencil in position and add the brown dot to each one. If you feel confident, you can do this freehand with a pointed artist's brush.

Border

The border is a running repeat and it won't matter if it runs off the ends. Or, it can continue around the edges.

1. Trace the entire design so you can cut several repeat patterns at one time. In this way your design elements will be perfectly spaced. (Alternative border designs are given at the end of this project.)

Blanket chest border stencil

15

2. Once cut, tape the stencil strip in position on the painted surface of your object.
3. Using the yellow paint, stencil the border design. Lift the stencil and reposition to continue the design.
4. Using a pointed artist's brush, pencil end, or Q-Tip, place a yellow dot in the center of each design. Save all paint until you have finished. In this way you can touch up any mistakes after you are through.

To finish

In order to protect the painted finish, you can give the entire piece a coat of varnish. I recommend a matte or dull finish. Let this dry overnight.

Alternative border design for blanket chest

Alternative border designs for blanket chest

Alternative border design for blanket chest

SPICE RACK

Borders can be used in small areas to enhance wooden items such as a spice rack, the front or sides of a bookshelf, or the drawers of a cabinet.

Try to incorporate handles or knobs into the design. For example, you might stencil a drawer front with flowers, using the round knobs for the centers, which are then surrounded by petals.

Materials

Fine sandpaper; latex or acrylic paint for background color (beige used here); 1-inch paintbrush; tracing paper; pencil; masking tape; X-acto craft knife; stencil paper; small tubes of white and deep-red acrylic paints; small stencil brushes; saucers or paper plates.

Directions

Remove all knobs or handles. If you are starting with raw wood, sand the surface smooth. Wipe away sand dust and paint the object. Let dry and paint again. Sand lightly. If you're using a wood stain, apply in the same way, allowing each coat to dry thoroughly.

Cutting the stencil

The floral designs used on top of the spice rack and on the drawer fronts are made from one pattern, which is then reversed. You will have to cut 2 stencils for this. And since this is a 2-color design, you will need a stencil for each color.

1. Trace the stem-and-leaf pattern, including the center of the flower, 2 times.
2. Cut a piece of stencil paper so that it will fit on the object to be stenciled. Place this over one of the traced designs and tape together.
3. Place this on a cutting surface and, using smooth strokes, cut out the stencil with your craft knife.
4. Turn the second traced stem-and-leaf design over and repeat step 3. You now have two reverse patterns of the same design.
5. Using a small piece of stencil paper, cut out the flower-petal stencil in the same manner by cutting each petal individually, leaving at least a 1-inch margin all around the circumference of the design.

Stenciling

1. Tape the flower-petal stencil in place over the area where you will later replace the knob on a drawer.
2. Squirt a small amount of white paint into a saucer or paper plate. Dip the end bristles of the stencil brush into the

paint and tap up and down on newspaper to remove excess paint. Your brush should be almost dry.

3. Hold the brush in an upright position and pounce up and down over the cut-out stencil area.

4. Lift the stencil and reposition it on the top front of the spice rack.

5. Now you can place the stem-and-leaf stencil (which includes center of flower) in position and stencil this with the deep-red color. Be sure to cover the previously stenciled white flower area so no red paint accidently touches it. Repeat on the corresponding side with the second stem-and-leaf stencil.

Border

The border design is a simple half-moon with a dot in the center.

1. Measure the area to be stenciled. Mark the exact dimensions of the area to be stenciled on the tracing paper and trace the border within this outline. Adjust the spacing to fit your object before cutting out the stencil.

2. Cut out 2 or 3 half-moons in position so that you have register marks for perfect balance. The dot within the design can be cut with a paper punch for a perfect circle.

3. Prepare the paint as before and tape the stencil in position. Cover the dot with masking tape and apply the paint.

4. Lift the stencil and reposition it so that one of the cutouts covers and perfectly matches a previously painted area. Continue to stencil the border in this way.

5. Remove the masking tape and mask out the half-moon. Position the stencil over each border element and apply a circle of white paint to each.

Large flower stencil for spice rack

Spice rack border design

UTENSIL HOLDER

Reproductions of Early American wooden objects such as a salt box or this utensil holder are quite popular for stencil design. If you can't find this exact item, consider crocks, tins, canisters, and such for a kitchen accessory. The design used here is adaptable for many shapes and sizes.

The bright yellow, orange, and green colors are especially pleasing for a modern kitchen, but if you prefer a country feeling, use more subdued or natural colors.

Materials

Wooden object; yellow, orange, brown, and green latex paints; 1-inch paintbrush; tracing paper; pencil; stencil paper; masking tape; X-acto knife; stencil brushes; saucers or paper plates.

Directions

Give the wooden object 2 coats of yellow paint inside and out. If you prefer, the inside can be painted a contrasting color.

Cutting the stencils

1. Trace the small flower-and-leaf stencil (A). Trace the large center flower (B) as one stencil, and the stem and leaves (C) as another.

Small flower stencil for utensil holder

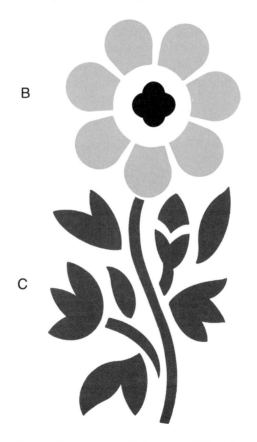

Large flower stencil for utensil holder

2. Tape a piece of stencil paper over the small design (A) and place this on a cutting surface.
3. With the X-acto knife, cut through each element. Make a stencil in the same way for the large flower petals, but do not cut out the center area. Be sure to leave approximately 1-inch margin around the cutout petals. Make another stencil for the stem and leaves (C).
4. Find the center of the front of the object and tape the stem-and-leaf stencil (C) down. Cut any excess paper from the bottom portion of the stencil sheet so that the design can lie flat.

Stenciling

1. Squirt a small amount of green paint onto a saucer or plate. If the color is too dark, add a drop of white to lighten it. Dip the stencil brush into the paint and tap up and down on newspaper to remove most of the paint. Stipple on the stencil, pouncing up and down with a firm hand.
2. Lift the stencil and reposition it in the center of one side of the wooden object. Stencil as before and repeat on the opposite side.
3. While you are using the green paint, you will move on to the stem and leaves of the smaller stencil (A). Mask out the flower with tape or paper. Tape the stencil on a slight angle to one side of the center design. Add green paint through the cutout area. Lift and repeat on the opposite side. Repeat on the sides of the holder as well.
4. Follow the diagram and stencil 3 stem-and-leaf designs (A) (with flowers still masked out) upside down on the top of the object. Place a leaf stencil at the very top where the stems meet.
5. Remove the masking tape and cover the stem and leaf areas.
6. With a clean brush, stencil the orange flowers of stencil (A) in place above each stem on all sides, front and top of the box.
7. Position the flower-petal stencil (B) over the center stem and leaves and apply orange paint as before. Be especially careful not to get orange paint on the green stem where the two colors meet. Repeat on each side.
8. Remove the stencil and retape it to the tracing. Then cut out the center hole.
9. Tape this design back in position on the object so that the petals are in perfect register. Apply brown paint to the center area. Remove stencil and repeat on each side.

   Note: If you prefer, you can stencil one of the alternative designs over the entire side panels of the utensil holder.

Two alternative side-panel designs for the utensil holder

COUNTRY PILLOWS

The technique for stenciling on fabric is the same as that done on wood, tin, etc. While acrylic paint is most often used in stenciling, there are special paints made for fabrics. These are called textile paints and are sold in art supply stores. They are absorbed by the fabric and are less opaque than acrylic paints.

The designs used for the country pillows are fashioned after Early American quilt patterns. The bright green and pink colors make the designs look contemporary. The finished size of each is 14 × 14 inches plus the border or ruffles.

Materials

For each pillow: 1/2 yard white cotton fabric; 1/2 yard green fabric for pillow back and borders; 2 1/2 yards of 2-inch-wide eyelet or lace trim, if desired; 2 1/2 yards of pink piping; tracing paper; pencil; stencil paper; masking tape; X-acto knife; stencil brushes; green, red, and white acrylic or textile paints; saucers or paper plates; 14-inch pillow form or Polyfil® stuffing.

Directions

To prepare Rose of Sharon and Country Basket pillows

1. Cut a 14 1/2-inch square from both the white fabric and the green fabric.
2. Cut two 2 1/2 × 15-inch and two 2 1/2 × 10 1/2-inch green strips for the border.

To prepare Tulip pillow

Cut a 15-inch square from white fabric and one from green fabric.

Preparing the stencils

Rose of Sharon pillow

1. This is a 2-color stencil with various elements. Trace each element so it can be cut out as an isolated stencil.
2. Fold the fabric in half vertically and horizontally and finger-press to create a crease. Open the fabric and fold diagonally from corner to corner in each direction to create an X crease. Open fabric. The design elements will be positioned on the crease lines.
3. Tape the white fabric square to a paper-padded surface so the fabric is taut.

Country pillow—Rose of Sharon design

Border for Rose of Sharon pillow

Cutting the stencils

1. Tape a piece of stencil paper over each tracing. Leave a margin of stencil paper around each design.
2. Using a craft knife, cut out each element with smooth, even strokes.
3. Cut enough of the border stencil so that it goes more than halfway down the side of the pillow.
4. Note that the flower (A-B) is made up of 2 separate stencils. Tape stencil (A) to the center of the fabric to begin.

Stenciling

1. Mix a bright pink color by adding a drop of white paint to a tablespoonful of red. Blend until there are no streaks in the paint. Prepare a dish with green paint as well.
2. With a small amount of paint on your brush, tap up and down on the stencil until the center flower cutout is filled in.
3. Remove the stencil when dry and set aside. Follow the diagram using the creased lines for placement and continue to stencil in the following sequence:

Stenciling sequence

1. Flower (A), green
2. Flower (B), bright pink
3. Stem with leaves (C), green
4. 7 buds around center flower (D), green
5. Flower buds in 3 corners opposite stem (E), bright pink
6. Border, bright pink
   Note that the border is not identical in all four corners.

When stenciling the corners to the right and left of the stem (C), mask out the adjoining cutouts with plain paper and stipple one design element as shown on the diagram.

Overlap to register first one corner and then the next.

Finish

With the right sides facing and raw edges aligned, stitch short green strips to the top

Layout for Rose of Sharon pillow

and bottom edge of the pillow top, leaving 1/4-inch seam allowances. Open and press seams from the back. With right sides facing, attach remaining strips to either side. Open and press.

Pin welting all around the pillow front so that the raw edges match. Using a zipper foot, stitch to the pillow top, overlapping the edges where they meet.

Pin the back square to the stenciled pillow top. Using previous stitches as a guide, sew around 3 sides and 4 corners with 1/4-inch seam allowance. Turn right side out and stuff. Slip stitch opening closed.

Tulip pillow

1. This is a 2-color, 2-stencil design. (See pages xi–xii.) Trace the design.
2. Cut out one stencil for the pink color (A) and another for the green (B).
3. Crease the fabric as for the Rose of Sharon pillow.
4. Beginning with the green stencil, position the stem in the corner on one diagonal crease. Stencil on the taut fabric as for the Rose of Sharon pillow.

5. Tape the stencil (A) in position so that it is in register and apply the pink paint by tapping up and down with an almost-dry brush.
6. Lift the stencil and repeat on the remaining three corners.

Finish

Attach the piping as for the Rose of Sharon pillow. With right sides facing, seam short ends of the ruffle strip together.

Divide the eyelet loop into four equal parts and mark with a pin.

With right sides facing and raw edges

Country pillow—Tulip pillow

aligned, gather and pin the eyelet to the pillow top. Sew around, following the stitch line.

Pin the ruffle toward the center of the pillow temporarily. Attach back piece and finish as for the Rose of Sharon pillow. Unpin the ruffles.

Country Basket pillow

There are 2 separate stencils for this design. Trace and cut each stencil piece. The design in each square of your creased fabric is identical.

1. Make a tracing of each design in position within a 15-inch square.

2. Use this as a guide to the exact placement of each stencil. The space between each border is the same width as the border strip.
3. Crease fabric vertically and horizontally.

Stencil sequence

Stencil the pink (A) first, in all 4 positions on the pillow. Next stencil the green (B) in all 4 positions on the pillow.

Finish

Add the border strips and piping the same as for the Rose of Sharon pillow. Attach backing, and then stuff.

Country Basket pillow

TILE TRIVET

Make your own expensive-looking decorative tiles with delicate floral stencils. The acrylic paint adheres to tile as well as to most other surfaces.

The trivet, made of four tiles preset in a wood frame, is a delightful and practical gift. The color scheme can be personalized and it takes minutes to finish. These items can be found in housewares and gift stores, or you can buy regular 4-inch-square ceramic bathroom tiles from a tile or hardware store. These can be used individually or you can set them into a wooden frame of the appropriate size.

It would be easy to adapt this repeat pattern for use on a piece of furniture such as a Parson's table, kitchen cabinets, a small dresser or night table, on a lampshade, even on a floor.

Materials

Glazed or unglazed tile or trivet; tracing paper; pencil; masking tape; 1-inch paintbrush; stencil paper; X-acto knife; stencil brushes; yellow, green, red, white, and black acrylic paints; paper plates (one for each color) or shallow dishes.

Directions

This trivet is made up of four 4-inch tiles. The stencil is made up of 5 repeats of the flower design in position to stencil on one tile. Each design is one color and they are far apart. Therefore it isn't necessary to mask out or cut separate stencils.

To begin, place a strip of masking tape over the tiles where they touch the wood frame. Using a bright yellow paint and your 1-inch paintbrush, paint the frame all around. When dry, remove the tape. If there is any paint on the tiles, it can be removed with warm water.

Cutting the stencils

1. Trace the complete design (all 5 elements) and tape stencil paper on top. Place this on a cutting surface.
2. If you want the buds and stems to be different colors, you will cut 2 separate stencils, one for each color. Then you must mask out each color as you stencil the other. The lines on the art are for positioning the stencil on one 4-inch tile.

Tile trivet stencil

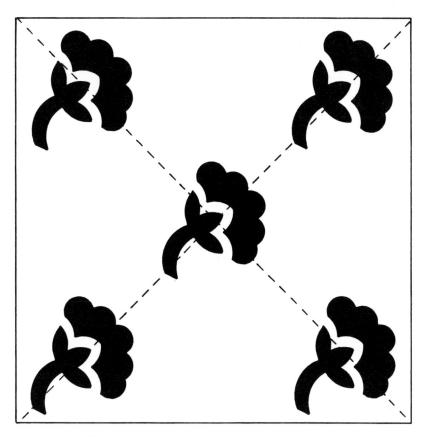

Diagram for positioning stencils

Stenciling

To mix the pastel pink color, add a drop of red to a tablespoon of white and combine until color is consistent. Add black to white in the same way to create a soft gray. Add green to white for a pastel green.

1. Position the stencil on one tile and tape at each corner.
2. The top left and bottom right corner designs are green. Stencil these first, using a small amount of pale green paint on your brush.
3. Next, stencil the bottom left and top right corners with pale pink.
4. With the stencil sheet still in position, stipple the gray paint onto the remaining center flower.
5. Remove the stencil and position it on the next tile as before. Continue until all four tiles are complete.

ALL-PURPOSE BOXES

These designs will fit a variety of objects. When used on 5- and 8-inch boxes, they fill the area nicely. Many of my readers write to say that stenciled boxes are good bazaar sellers and are easy and fun to make. You can either paint the insides or line each with pretty paper or fabric. As a Christmas gift, a velvet-lined box is perfect for jewelry.

Materials

Hinged wooden box; tracing paper; pencil; stencil paper; X-acto knife; 1-inch paintbrush; yellow, red, and green acrylic paints (tomato box); purple, white, and green acrylic paints (berry box); stencil brushes; saucers or paper plates; lining (optional); felt for bottom (optional).

Directions

Paint the yellow box inside and out. If you plan to line the box, you will only paint the inside rim. Set aside to dry. To achieve the lavender color, mix a drop of purple paint into a pool of white paint and mix thoroughly. Add either more white or more color to reach the desired shade. Paint the box.

Cutting the stencil

1. Trace each stencil design. Place a piece of stencil paper over each on a cutting surface. Since each design is a 2-color stencil, you will cut 2 stencils for each, one for the green leaves, another for berries or tomato. (See pages xi–xii.)
2. Make 2 separate tracings of each design to use as a placement guide.

Begin by using the uncut tracing of each design to position your stencil. To do this, place the tracing on the box so that the design flows from the top to the front of the box. Crease the paper on the top edge so it will stay in position temporarily.

1. Squirt a small amount of green paint onto a flat dish.
2. Place the stem-and-leaf stencil for each design over the tracing in position on the box, and carefully remove the tracing paper from underneath. Tape the stencil to the box.
3. Tap the stencil brush on the paint and then tap on newspaper a few times to remove excess paint. It is important to apply the paint almost dry, especially over a corner or curved area.
4. Hold the stencil paper flat against the box with one hand. In the other, hold the brush perpendicular to the surface with your elbow firmly positioned on the table. Tap the color onto the area.
5. When the paint is dry, replace the tracing in position as a guide for registering the second stencil. Place the second stencil over the tracing, carefully re-

All-purpose boxes

move the tracing paper, and tape down the stencil.

6. Using the red paint, complete the tomato stencil design. Using the purple paint, complete the berry design.

Finish

To line the boxes

Paper lining

Measure all inside walls and bottom. When cutting out paper (wrapping, contact, or wall paper can be used), add 1/2 inch to all dimensions.

Using white glue, affix all sides first. They will overlap at the corners. Any excess paper that extends beyond the top rim can be trimmed with a razor blade.

Set the bottom piece in last. The slight excess will extend up to cover the inside edges all around.

Fabric lining

If lining with felt, cut all pieces exact size to measurement. Glue in position.

When using fabrics that fray, cut each piece slightly larger than measurement. Cut a piece of thin cardboard for each section so it is approximately 1/4 inch *smaller* than each measurement.

Spread glue over each cardboard piece and center it to the wrong side of the corresponding fabric piece, glue side down. Spread a small amount of glue over the back of the cardboard and fold the fabric edges over to glue in place. Add a little glue to the fabric that has been turned to the back and set each side piece in position in the box.

Press tightly to set the piece. Repeat with the inside bottom piece last. Add a piece of paper or felt to the outside bottom of the box to finish.

KITCHEN PLAQUE

Designing with words

The size of the letters and the number of words in a saying determine the design. If you use graph paper to plan the layout, you can figure out the best way to stencil a saying on any size object.

Stenciled letters come precut and in many styles and sizes. You can find them in most variety stores.

Breadboards can be found in hardware or five-and-dime stores, or you can use a wooden plaque, available in a variety of sizes. Framed fabric is another background often used for a stenciled saying.

Materials

Breadboard or other appropriate background material; tracing paper; pencil; precut stencil letters (optional); masking tape; stencil paper; X-acto knife; 1-inch paintbrush; stencil brushes; yellow, red, navy blue, and green acrylic paints; saucers or paper plates.

Directions

Begin by making a rough sketch on tracing paper. Draw the outline of the breadboard; then draw the words in position through the stencil letters to make up each line of the saying. (To cut your own stencil letters, trace them from the book and, following *Border* directions, cut each one.)

Using the 1-inch brush, paint the front surface of the breadboard with yellow acrylic paint. Let dry and paint again if needed. Paint the rim all around with green paint. Let dry.

Draw a line down the center of the board. Draw light pencil lines, evenly spaced for each line of the saying, beginning with the line for the upside-down heart. Or, you can place 6 strips of masking tape, evenly spaced, above which you will stencil each word.

Count the number of letters in each word, divide by 2, and space them accordingly to the right and left of the drawn center line. Since each letter is different, it is difficult to space them perfectly. However, this can be done fairly accurately by eye and the end result will look perfect.

To cut the letters

If you are not using precut stencil letters, trace each letter to be used. Tape a piece of stencil paper over each and place on a cutting surface. Carefully cut out each letter of the saying.

Stenciling

1. Beginning with the letter O, hold the stencil to the left of the vertical line and resting on the second horizontal line.

Kitchen plaque layout

2. Dip your brush lightly into the navy blue paint and tap up and down on newspaper before stenciling the letter on the breadboard. Tap the brush up and down to stencil the letter.
3. Let dry, then carefully remove the stencil. Next, place the letter M to the right of the vertical line opposite the O and continue to stencil in this way. Every other line is green, alternating with navy blue.

   Note: Stencil letters may require touch-ups. Save the paint until the project is finished. If you place a wet paper towel over the dish the paint won't dry out.

Border

1. Trace the 4 hearts in a row.
2. Tape the stencil paper over the tracing on a cutting surface and cut out the hearts with a sharp craft knife. A rounded design such as this is hard to make perfectly smooth; however, when stenciled, it will look like a perfectly drawn design.
3. Center the complete design on your board along the bottom line with 2 hearts on either side of the drawn vertical line.
4. Using red paint, stencil each heart to make up the border.
5. Turn the stencil upside down and stencil one heart in the center of the top line on the board (see diagram).

Kitchen plaque stencil

SALT BOX

In colonial times salt was kept in a small box hanging in the kitchen. The stenciled decoration reflects the colonial practice of decorating small pieces. The schoolhouse design is a familiar one often used for quilt appliqués. It is quite fitting for this wooden object which is a readily available reproduction of the original.

Materials

Small wooden box; tracing paper; pencil; masking tape; stencil paper; X-acto knife; 1-inch paintbrush; red, white, blue, and yellow acrylic paints; stencil brushes; saucers or paper plates.

Directions

Mix the pink background color by adding a drop at a time of red paint to white. Apply a coat or two as needed.

1. Trace the schoolhouse design.
2. Tape the stencil paper over the tracing and cut out the design.
3. Remove the stencil sheet and tracing. Cut a second stencil of the windows in position as they will appear on the schoolhouse.

Stenciling

1. Center the house stencil on the top of the box and tape in position.
2. Using a small amount of blue paint on your brush, stipple the color onto the background until the area is filled in.
3. Remove the stencil and reposition it on the front panel, aligned under the previous stencil. Apply the color. Repeat on each side.
4. Remove the stencil and place the window stencil in position on the already stenciled schoolhouse. Be sure it's centered correctly.
5. Apply a small amount of yellow paint over the blue paint to each of the 3 cutout areas. Repeat on each side.

Finish

You can paint or line the inside with pretty paper to finish. (See page 34 on how to do this.) Hang on the wall for a country accent in your kitchen.

Salt box schoolhouse motif

PASTEL PILLOWS

When using five or six different stencils on three different items, preplanning is important. If you figure out the steps to doing all the items beforehand, the actual stenciling will go quickly and easily.

These stencils can be used on a variety of accessories and they will look entirely different depending on how you place them. For example, if you make a tablecloth, use the leaves as a border with a flower in the center. Or place the flowers at random. The possibilities are limitless. These are prettiest when pastel colors are used.

Materials

For each pillow: 2 pieces white cotton (or cotton blend) fabric 16 × 16 inches; 2 yards each of welting in one of the paint colors; 1/2-inch-wide lace trim; 3-inch-wide ruffled eyelet (eyelet is dyed to match stencil colors); 14-inch pillow form, or Polyfil® stuffing; tracing paper; pencil; X-acto knife; stencil paper; stencil brushes; blue, green, red, white, and mustard-color acrylic paints; paper plates or saucers.

Directions

Pillow tops
(Pillow A) Baste a 12-inch square, centered on a 16-inch square pillow top.

Cutting the stencils

1. Trace the design as one stencil and cut a piece of stencil paper an inch or so larger all around than the design. Center stencil paper over the pattern. Tape together and place on a cutting surface.
2. Cut out each design element. Since this is a 2-color stencil, the color not being used will be masked out when stenciling the other color. Simply tape a piece of paper over these areas. (See pages xi–xii.)
3. Place the fabric on a hard surface. Using Pillow A layout as a guide, tape the stencil in position within the marked area.

   Note: Since fabric painting is permanent, practice on a scrap of fabric before doing it on the pillow.

Stenciling

1. Begin with the green leaves (with flowers masked out) and, using a dry brush, lightly dip it into the paint. Tap the brush up and down on newspaper, then

Pillows A & C

Pillow C

Pillow C

Stencil elements for flower pillows

Pillows A & C

Pillows B & C

Pillows B & C

Stencil elements for flower pillows

onto the fabric, stippling, not brushing, in a firm up-and-down motion. To darken the color or create shading, go over the same area several times, always using a nearly dry brush. Finish with one color, then clean and dry the brush thoroughly before starting another color.

2. When dry, remove the stencil and masking, and then mask out the cutout stem and leaf areas. Retape the stencil in position so that the previously stenciled areas are in register. This will ensure proper placement of the flowers.

3. To mix the pink color, squirt a small amount of white into a dish and add a pin-size drop of red. Mix thoroughly and add a drop more of color at a time, if needed. Since each flower section is a different color, be sure to clean the stencil sheet after each application and use a new or cleaned brush for each color.

Pillow tops
(Pillow B) Baste a 13½-inch square centered on a 16-inch pillow top.

To stencil

1. Trace and cut out the leaf design.
2. Mask out the teardrop shape and stencil the leaf motif just inside the basted lines to make the border.
3. For the middle flower, trace and cut out the appropriate design element. Stencil the leaves first, then the flower, as for Pillow A.

4. Using the red paint, create shading by applying a second and third stippling to the center areas of each cutout flower shape. Go over this as many times as needed to achieve the desired effect.

5. Reposition the border stencil, remove the masking paper, and apply red paint to the teardrop all around. Be careful to keep red paint in the cutout area only.

Pillow tops
(Pillow C) (Center) This pillow is made up of a combination of all the designs. Refer to the diagram for placement. These flowers can be placed at random, leaving about 1½ inches unpainted along each side of the pillow top.

Assembly

Remove basting stitches. With right sides up, stitch trims to pillow tops in this order: piping, narrow ruffle, wide eyelet ruffle.

Place pillow back over front of pillow top with raw edges matching. Stitch around three sides and four corners. Turn right side out and stuff. Slip stitch open edges closed.

Note: I've included two other pillow designs for you to choose from (page 48). One is an all-over design and one can be used on each of the four corners of a pillow top.

Pillow C

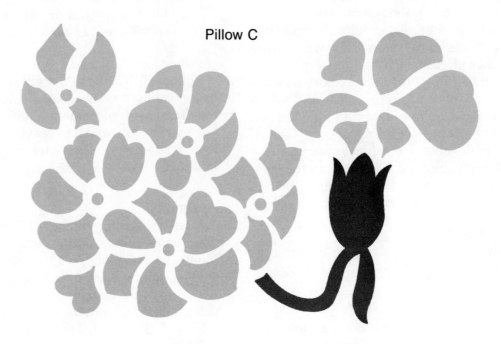

Additional stencil element

Layout for Pillow A

Layout for Pillow B

Layout for Pillow C

Alternative pillow layouts

PLATE 7   Holiday Door Decoration

PLATE 8   Holiday Table Setting

PLATE 9   Cookie Tins, Oval
Boxes

PLATE 10   Holiday Tray,
Greeting Cards, Wrapping
Paper, and Gift Tags

PLATE 11   Boat Cushions

PLATE 12   Flowerpot, Heart Boxes, Gift Bags, Flower Basket

PLATE 13   *Welcome Plaque, Child's Step Stool, Baby Pillow, and Country Accessories*

Book Two

First Steps in Stenciling Gifts and Holiday Decorations

Special occasions give us one more excuse for crafting. Whether it's making gifts for others or something for ourselves, nothing gets us going like a coming event. The birth of a new baby is cause for celebration with a gift. A wedding, anniversary, birthday, and certainly Christmas have us reaching into the sewing basket, checking new fabrics, looking through magazines for fresh ideas. It is at these times that we like to give a special gift, one that we will be remembered for when the gift is used. There is nothing as personal or appreciated as a handmade gift. By taking everyday items, designing them in a pretty way and adding the personal touch of a color or design motif that is just right for the person, it is given and received with more feeling than one which has been purchased.

Christmastime often brings out the creative urge in all of us, even if we don't make anything at any other time of the year. Our homes seem to cry out for sprucing up to add to the holiday spirit.

Stenciling is the perfect craft for the busy person who wants quick, good-looking results. It's a wonderful way to turn a plain, store-bought gift into something special.

When it comes to ornaments, gift tags, greeting cards, and wrapping paper, stenciling is the ideal craft. Because it takes more time to prepare the stencil than the actual crafting, it is practical to make several projects at once. In this way, once a stencil is cut you can use it over and over, varying the placement and arrangement or using it on various items.

The holiday tray, for example, was designed with several stencils to make up the whole. Each relates to the other but is complete by itself. Therefore it is easy to see how they look alone. Each gift tag is made from a different stencil to create variety. Your stationery will be personalized if you use one, or part of a design, in a corner or as a border by repeating it across or around the sheet.

The Christmas trees used as borders on placemats and a table runner can also be used on three-dimensional objects such as a canister or recipe box. It's easy to enlarge this design (see pages x–xi) so that you can have one large tree on the object rather than a group that creates a border.

Many of the designs can be used in different colors. For example, the red cookie tins have white designs while the same bird and Noel greetings are softened in a pastel theme. Each is equally delightful and makes your homemade treats more festive.

When you make special items to be brought out at holiday time it's particularly meaningful. Each year you will remember Christmases past. Perhaps you will even pass these handmade treasures on to your children, thus adding to the nostalgic aura of childhood.

Also included in this section are gift ideas suitable for birthdays, housewarming, and other special occasions.

3

HOLIDAY DOOR DECORATION

Almost any kind of square or flat-back container can be used as a door decoration once stenciled and filled with greens. An open wooden box with a simple design can be just right.

This red-and-green stencil of holly, berries, and a ribbon is a popular Christmas design. The grid of hearts on each side is a nice addition often used as a country motif.

Materials

Wooden object; tracing paper; pencil; stencil paper; masking tape; X-acto knife; red, green, and white acrylic paints; 1-inch paintbrush; stencil brush; saucers or paper plates.

Directions

Since this is a 2-color stencil with colors practically touching, you will cut two separate stencils with register guides. (See pages xi–xii.) This means that when cutting the bow-and-berry stencil, you will cut a little bit of the leaves as well. And when you cut the leaf stencil, you will cut part of the berries or bow for exact placement of each color.

Begin by painting the wooden box with white acrylic paint. Let dry and coat again.

Sometimes white paint requires three coats before it is completely opaque. If so, apply another coat. Acrylic paint dries quickly.

Cutting the stencil

1. Trace the entire design as it will appear.
2. Tape the stencil paper over the tracing and place on a hard surface.
3. Using the craft knife, cut out the bow, ribbon streamers, and berries. To cut perfect circles you can use a paper punch. However, it might be just as easy to leave the stencil in place and cut out the circles with the knife. They will appear almost perfectly round when stenciled and look more real. Cut a small portion of a leaf. Remove the cut stencil from the tracing.
4. Place another stencil sheet over the traced design (part of which has been cut away) and cut out the leaves and a small portion of the bow.
5. Cut the stencil for the smaller berry design in the same manner.

Stenciling

1. Determine where the design will go and tape the ribbon/berry stencil to the box. Mask out the small portion of the cutout leaf with a piece of tape.
2. Using a small amount of red paint, tap

Door decoration stencils

your brush up and down on newspaper until it is almost dry. Then begin to fill the area with an up-and-down pouncing of the brush. Remove the stencil and take the masking away from the covered section.

3. Position the second stencil so that the register marks correspond with part of the already stenciled design. Mask out the red area with tape. With a clean brush, stencil the green areas as you did the red.

4. Stencil the smaller berry design in the same manner.

Side Panel

A repeat design such as the grid pattern of hearts on the sides of the box represents an overall design that can be used on any background. Though hearts were used for this par-

ticular door decoration, you can use any of the design motifs shown.

Cutting the stencil

1. Trace the series of hearts or design element that you've chosen in place. This is a pattern that will fit any small item.

2. Tape the stencil paper over the tracing and place on a cutting surface.

3. Using your craft knife, cut out each small design. Tiny stencils don't have to be perfect. It is almost impossible to cut a small stencil with great accuracy. But even if it is crooked or uneven, it will look fine as part of a pattern.

4. Use this stencil as a whole to move from one section to the next. In this way, if your object is larger, a table, for example, the design will fit because the grid has been worked out so that all the designs are evenly spaced.

Designs for use on door decoration

Additional designs to use on door decoration

Stenciling

1. Using the placement layout as a guide, tape the stencil in position and fill each area with a small amount of red paint on your brush. Use an up-and-down pouncing motion.
2. Lift the stencil and reposition it, using the previously stenciled hearts to register the design. This is why you have cut several hearts rather than repeating the one. The designs are now perfectly spaced and in register.

3. Continue to fill the surface with the overall pattern.

Finish

If the box is to be used on an exterior door, give it a coat or two of varnish to protect the surface. This can be spray varnish which dries quickly but is less effective than the long-drying varnish, or polyurethane.

Fill the box with an arrangement of greens, add a red bow if desired, and hang on your door.

Use this placement layout diagram to create diagonal grid on door decoration

HOLIDAY TABLE SETTING

Canvas place mats, table runners, and floor cloths have always been popular stencil items. The material is sturdy and easy to stencil and the oatmeal color has a nice country look. Almost any color shows up well against this texture.

The graphic Christmas tree shapes make a wonderful repeat border in this one-color stencil. Nothing could be easier for a last-minute project. The mats would make wonderful bazaar items.

Materials

Heavy canvas or muslin (for precut runners and place mats, see source list, pages ix–x); tracing paper; pencil; craft knife; stencil paper; stencil brush; green acrylic paint; saucer.

Directions

If you are making your own runner and place mats, determine the sizes to best fit on your table. Make generous hems to accommodate the design, or fringe the edges.

Cutting the stencil

Place mat
Trace the smaller tree design. You may want to cut two stencils side by side or one above the other to ensure perfect placement. However, this isn't necessary if you are careful when lining up the border.

1. Place the stencil paper over the tracing and tape them together. Place on a cutting surface.
2. With the craft knife, cut out the tree design.

Stenciling

1. Measure in approximately 1½–2 inches from each side edge of the mat and make light pencil lines down the sides to indicate where the first border will be placed.
2. Center and tape the stencil in position over the top of the first marked line beginning about ½ inch from the top edge of the mat.
3. Using a small amount of bright green paint on your brush, fill in the stencil. As you apply the paint, use greater pressure on the brush to achieve a dark tone, but do not load the brush with paint.
4. Lift the stencil and reposition it directly under the design you have just finished. Make sure to check your pencil guideline to keep the border of trees perfectly straight.
5. When one vertical line of trees is complete, make the second line so that there will be approximately ½ inch between the two rows of trees. Again, accuracy is

important to the finished design. Set the paint aside and cover with a damp paper towel if necessary to keep from drying out while you prepare the runner.

Runner

Trace the larger tree design and prepare the stencil as you did before, leaving a 2-inch margin of stencil paper under the design.

1. Measure approximately 1½ to 2 inches up from the bottom edge of the runner and cut the excess stencil paper under the design to line up perfectly with the runner edge.
2. Tape the stencil in position on the fabric and stencil with the bright green paint.
3. As you reposition the stencil to create the border, check to be sure your distancing is consistent. Repeat along top edge in the same way.

This design is a good one to use on Christmas cards, cookie tins, recipe boxes, and other gift items. Use it in reverse as well; a white stencil on a green background.

Holiday table setting stencils

COOKIE TINS AND OVAL BOXES

If you're planning to give baked goodies to friends and relatives, make it extra special with a stenciled container. The tins come in a variety of colors and sizes and all you do is add the design.

When baking for the church bazaar, this is a good way to present the cookies and cakes. Once the stencil is cut you can whip up a batch of containers in an afternoon.

Materials

A variety of tins; tracing paper; pencil; masking tape; stencil paper; precut stencil letters to fit your tin tops; X-acto knife; white, red, and green acrylic paints; stencil brushes; saucers or paper plates.

Directions

Since the tins are already painted, you have a smooth surface on which to apply a design. However, because the paint is so slick, it is harder to apply the acrylic paint so that it is opaque. When using white on red,

for example, you will have to repeat the stencil application several times before removing the stencil.

Cutting the stencil

1. Trace the bird design. This is a one-color stencil and will be cut as a single design.
2. Tape the stencil paper over the tracing and, using the X-acto knife, cut out each element. Leave a margin of stencil paper around the design, especially where you have cut the fragile stem and leaves.
3. Place the tin on tracing paper and mark around the curve with a pencil. Trace each of the letters of N O E L onto the tracing inside the curved area to see how the spacing will look. Adjust to fit and determine where the bird will appear.

Stenciling

1. Tape the bird stencil in position on the tin and stencil with a small amount of white paint.
2. Tap up and down many times. As you do this the red will still show through the paint. Do not overload your brush. Simply let the paint dry for a minute or two and reapply the paint using the same, almost dry brush.
3. Remove the stencil and, using your stencil as a guide, position each letter on the tin.

Cookie tin stencil

Oval box stencil

4. Hold in place with one hand while stippling with the brush in the other. The shape of the tin and the stencil sheet of letters make it awkward to tape each letter in position. Do not let the stencil slip out of register as you add paint. This is an area where it's important not to have too much paint on your brush, as it will smear under the stencil.

OVAL BOXES

These are nesting oval wooden boxes, used to hold baked goods or small gifts. Each can be filled with greens or Christmas ornaments for a holiday centerpiece.

To create a country feeling and for a change from traditional Christmas colors, paint them with pastels. The tops are white, but the sides are pale green with pink inside.

Materials

Oval boxes; tracing paper; pencil; masking tape; 1-inch brush; white, green, and red acrylic paints; stencil paper; stencil brushes; X-acto knife; saucers or paper plates.

Directions

Since this is a 2-color design with the colors touching, you will cut 2 stencils. The bell design is repeated on an oval box. This is a good example of how to make one design work in different ways.

1. Trace the ribbon and bell clapper. Tape a piece of stencil paper over the tracing, place on a cutting surface, and cut the stencils. Be sure there is enough paper around the stencil to keep paint off the surrounding tin.
2. Repeat with a new piece of stencil paper for the bell shape. Tape the bell stencil in position on the tin.
3. Add a drop of green paint to a tablespoonful of white paint and mix thoroughly.
4. Apply the pale green paint to the stencil cutout with an almost dry brush. Let dry and remove the stencil.

5. Place the bow stencil in position above the bell. You can do this by eye.
6. Add a drop of red paint to a tablespoon of white paint and mix thoroughly. Apply the pink color to the stencil area. Repeat for the clapper, taking care to place it as indicated (in a ringing position).

Adding the letters

Use precut stencil letters from the five-and-dime store or art store.

1. Trace the shape of the top of the tin or box.
2. Trace each letter through the cutout stencils so they are evenly spaced within the curve of the outline.
3. Place this over the stenciled tin to see how the message will look.
4. Using the tracing as a guide, slip the first letter, N, under the tracing and line it up before removing the tracing guide.
5. When stenciling N O E L on the tin with the bell, alternate paint colors for each letter. Always use a clean brush for each new color. Continue to stencil each letter using the tracing as a placement guide.

HOLIDAY TRAY

Whether it's a tin or wooden tray, this is the perfect stencil project. Each time you serve guests you'll be proud of its unique, handmade quality. This tray is designed with colorful symbols of Christmastime in the country tradition. The rocking horse is an enchanting, early design, reminiscent of childhood toys, the fruit and schoolhouse are often used in country decorating, and the goose and basket are simple designs sometimes found on quilts. The size of this tray is approximately 16 × 20 inches.

Materials

Tray; tracing paper; pencil; 1/2-inch masking tape; 1-inch paintbrush; Shaker blue, yellow, red, green, navy blue, and ivory acrylic paint; stencil paper; stencil brushes; X-acto knife; paper plates; spray varnish.

Directions

Begin by painting the entire tray with Shaker blue. Let dry and apply another coat. Let this dry thoroughly.

Mask out lines in the following way: Run a strip of tape along all four inside edges of the tray. Run two more strips of tape vertically on the tray with 4 inches between. Then run two strips horizontally across the tray with 4 inches between.

Stipple the paint over each marked-off square with ivory paint. Give this 2 or 3 coats to cover. Carefully peel away the masking tape.

Cutting the stencils

Each design is cut in a different way, depending on the number of colors used. For example, the apple and pear are 2-color designs and require 2 separate stencils, as do the schoolhouse and basket. However, the goose is made up of 4 stencils. The rocking horse is one color, but needs bridges when cutting. (See page xi.)

1. Trace each design.
2. Cut a 4-inch square of stencil paper for each design.
3. Center the stencil paper square over each design and tape together. Cut each element for each design in position on the 4-inch square.
4. Make a new tracing of each complete design to use as a register guide.

Stenciling

Mix the colors needed for each stencil on paper plates. You'll need a small amount of each color.

1. Locate the position of all the green stems and leaves for the apples and

pears. Tape or hold one stencil in place on the tray. Using a small amount of green paint on your brush, tap up-and-down onto the stencil. Lift the stencil sheet and reposition on another square. Make sure the paint from the first stencil has not seeped onto the underside of the stencil. If so, clean this with a damp cloth before proceeding.

2. Repeat for the other stem-and-leaf stencils while using the green paint. *Note:* A third apple uses another color combination of yellow for the apple and blue for the leaves. However, you can use the green and red here if desired.

3. While using green paint, stencil the basket A onto one square of the tray.

4. Next, use the red paint to stencil all the apples, stencil A of the schoolhouse, stencil A of the goose.

5. Using yellow, stencil the pears and the center apple. Stencil B of the goose using the tracing guide to locate the stencil position.

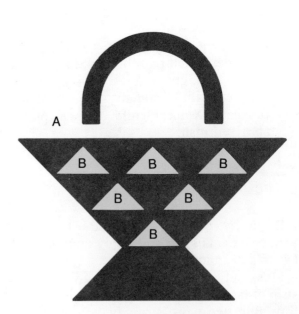

Holiday tray stencils

16

6. Next, stencil all remaining elements with blue paint. Lift the rocking horse stencil and touch up the areas where the bridges masked out the color. Position the roof B on the schoolhouse and the neck and bottom of the goose.

7. Place the schoolhouse stencil C over the design on the tray and stencil the windows with white paint. You may need 2 or 3 applications of white to sufficiently cover the area.

8. Place the basket stencil B in position (using the tracing guide) and stipple with white paint. Again, you will probably have to reapply the white to block out the green color beneath.

Finish

To protect the painted decorations, apply several coats of spray varnish. This will create a shiny, hard finish.

Glue a piece of felt to the bottom of the tray to protect your tabletop.

CHRISTMAS CARDS

If you've ever received a handmade Christmas card, you know how much more you appreciate and admire it than one that was purchased.

It's a cinch to make your own stenciled cards, and the designs and colors can be of your own choosing. You can make all that you need in one evening. It's fun to see them all together, so perfectly professional-looking, which is one of the rewards of this craft.

With cards becoming so costly, many people have stopped sending them, even though they'd like to extend their good wishes. Making your own cards is a good way to solve the problem beautifully.

Materials

Blank greeting cards and envelopes (art stores); tracing paper; pencil; masking tape; stencil paper; X-acto knife; stencil brushes; red, green, blue, yellow, and white acrylic paints; paper plates.

Directions

Notice that the stencil designs for the cards are all used together to create the serving tray, but when used on cards they look quite different. Practice before doing the final stenciling.

1. Trace the designs of your choice and tape a stencil sheet over each on a cutting board.
2. Using your craft knife, cut each color as a separate stencil.
3. Make a new tracing of each design to use as a register guide for the placement of each color.

Stenciling

1. Squirt small amounts of each paint color on paper plates. You can either use a different brush for each color, or wash and dry your brush thoroughly after working with each color.
2. Use the tracing of a design to position

each element of a stencil. It's easier to stencil several card designs at once by stenciling the common colors within each design, rather than completing one design in many colors.

3. Before applying paint to each area, mask off the previously painted section where two colors touch. Each time you get ready to apply color, slide the stencil paper under the tracing to locate the position of the cutout on your blank card. Hold the stencil in position, remove the tracing paper, and pounce up-and-down with an almost dry brush.

4. If you want to add a design to your envelopes as well, use the small stencils to create a design in one corner or on the back.

Greeting card stencils

19

Greeting card stencils

CHRISTMAS WRAPPING PAPER

It's fun and easy to make your own wrapping paper from one repeat stencil pattern. The Christmas trees look cheerful when stenciled in green on shiny white paper. If you buy rolls of white shelf paper, this is an inexpensive way to have well-designed packages. One paper is white with green trees; the other is blue with white trees.

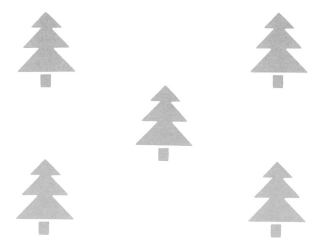

Wrapping paper stencil

Materials

Solid-color wrapping paper; tracing paper; pencil; masking tape; X-acto knife; white or green acrylic paint; small stencil brush; saucer.

Directions

1. Trace the design in a pattern of 6 or 8 trees.
2. Tape the stencil paper over the tracing on a cutting surface. Use the X-acto knife to cut out the designs. Use this pattern as one stencil to move over the paper. All trees will be evenly spaced and in register because you always have a stenciled design over which to place a cutout before continuing to stencil.
3. Spread the sheet of wrapping paper on a tabletop and tape lightly at each corner.
4. Place the cutout stencil in the upper left-hand corner but do not tape down, as this will ruin the paper.
5. Squirt a small amount of acrylic paint in a saucer and dip your brush into it so you have a little paint on the ends of the bristles. Tap up-and-down on newspaper.
6. Hold the stencil firmly in place and pounce the brush up-and-down over each cutout area. It takes no time to cover the entire pattern.
7. When it dries, lift the stencil and reposition it to the right, moving across the paper. Find a register mark by placing the stencil over one of the already stenciled

trees and continue to apply paint in this way. Cover the entire paper. Decorate enough paper to wrap all your packages.

Finish

Set the paint aside for making gift tags, notepaper, or greeting cards.

When the stenciled paper is dry, wrap your packages. Many of the other designs can be used to create wrapping paper. You can mix and match designs or create patterns with the designs. Have fun experimenting. This is a good project for which you can try a variety of design ideas.

Alternative wrapping paper designs

GIFT TAGS AND ORNAMENTS

Make a batch of gift tags from colorful poster board and a few stencils. You can cut them in any size or shape, punch a hole in each, and tie them on packages or use them as tree ornaments. This is a great way to let the kids help decorate the tree with their own creations.

Materials

Poster board in a variety of colors; tracing paper; pencil; masking tape; stencil paper; X-acto knife; assortment of acrylic paint colors; small stencil brushes; paper plates.

Directions

1. Leaving a few inches between each, trace a bunch of the small designs and tape a piece of stencil paper over them on a cutting surface.
2. Cut each one out with the craft knife.
3. Let the kids have fun stenciling each design several times on different-colored backgrounds. Leave enough room around each design for the tag outline. Squirt small amounts of different paint colors on paper plates. Hold the stencil down and apply the colors of your choice wherever you want. Where two colors touch, mask out one color with a piece of tape while you stencil the other. When it dries, remove the tape and cover the area on the cutout that was just stenciled. Continue in this way, making sure to leave enough space around each design to cut a shape for your tags and ornaments.
4. Trace each of the tag shapes provided here and tape the tracing over the stenciled designs.
5. Use your craft knife to cut the shape from the cardboard right through the tracing.
6. Use a paper punch to make a hole in the corner of each and tie with 1/4-inch satin ribbon, embroidery thread, or yarn.

Gift tags

BOAT CUSHIONS

If you have a friend who takes you sailing, the blue-and-white boat cushions would be a thoughtful gift. The design is created in such a way as to be adaptable on a variety of items. These are vinyl cushions, inexpensively purchased, that have been personalized. The project is a good example of how you might buy a plain, everyday item and give it gift status with a stencil.

Materials

Vinyl cushions; tracing paper; pencil; masking tape; stencil paper; X-acto knife; white and royal blue acrylic paints; stencil brushes; saucers or paper plates.

Directions

The only area to be particularly careful with when stenciling a border is the corners. This border will fit any size item. If the pillow is long and narrow, the border will still fit. If the item you're stenciling is larger, you simply extend or repeat the pattern to fit.

The vinyl material takes acrylic paint well. Since it is waterproof, this is a good outdoor item.

Preparing the design

1. Draw a rectangle the same size as your cushion on the tracing paper and plan the design to fit within.
2. Make a tracing of the corner design and position it to fit within the rectangle. Be sure that the border design is centered on the cushion and each corner design is in the same position equidistant from the drawn lines.
3. Trace the outline of the entire border twice before cutting the stencil. Set one tracing aside.
4. Trace the anchor design.

Cutting the stencil

1. Tape the stencil sheet over the traced designs and place on the cutting surface.
2. When cutting the stencil, make sure your craft knife is sharp to avoid choppiness when going around the curves of the rope design. Cut out one corner and a little more than half the border on each side of the corner. In this way you can line up the stencil in register when continuing the border lines. Make sure that the loops are on the outside of the square.
3. Cut the anchor in the same way.

Boat cushion border and anchor stencils

Stenciling

1. Tape the uncut tracing of the design over the cushion on the top two corners so you can lift the paper from the bottom.
2. Slide the stencil under the tracing so it corresponds in position. Lift the tracing out of the way and tape the stencil to the cushion.
3. Use a small amount of white paint on the blue background, and royal blue paint on the white. Dip a dry brush into the paint and stipple the area.

   Since you are working on a pliable surface, there is some give. Hold the stencil against the cushion as best you can, but be sure your brush isn't wet with paint or you won't have clean, sharp lines.
4. As the paint dries, lift the stencil and move it down to continue the border. Line the stencil up with a portion of the already-stenciled border so that you can continue a perfectly straight line.

5. When you reach the next corner, turn the stencil to position it. Before applying paint, place the tracing back over the cushion to be sure the corner is in the exact right place. Continue until finished.
6. Center the anchor stencil on the cushion. Hold it in position and stencil as for the border.

The palm tree and helm are alternative designs and can be used in the center of the cushions in place of the anchor.

Alternate boat cushion designs

28

GIFT BAG

Turn a plain piece of muslin into a delightful and decorative gift bag for a small object, or a container to hold potpourri.

As you see here, small stencils such as hearts, stars, or farm animals can be used to stencil an overall pattern on the fabric.

Materials

A piece of muslin 11 × 14 inches; 1/2 yard of 1/4-inch-wide pink satin ribbon; tracing paper; pencil; masking tape; stencil paper; X-acto knife; small stencil brushes; green, pink, blue, and white acrylic paints; piece of cardboard; paper plates or saucers.

Directions

Cutting the stencils

1. Trace 3 hearts evenly spaced in a row as shown.
2. Tape stencil paper over the heart tracing and cut out each heart with the craft knife.
3. On the stencil paper draw a line 1/2 inch above and below the hearts and cut away excess stencil paper.

Stenciling

1. Squirt a small amount of each color onto a plate and mix a drop of white into each. Blend until there are no streaks.
2. Tape the piece of muslin to a piece of cardboard on a tabletop.
3. Dip the stencil brush into one color of paint and tap up-and-down on newspaper to remove some of the paint.
4. Starting at one end of the fabric, hold the stencil cutout down and stipple the brush up-and-down on the heart openings. Be careful not to get paint on the fabric above and below the stencil paper. If this is difficult, place a piece of paper over the fabric adjacent to the areas you're stenciling.
5. Continue to stencil across the fabric to create a row of hearts. As you move the stencil, register the previous heart so you are always working on 2, not 3, new hearts.
6. Position the stencil for the next row so that the top of the stencil paper touches the bottom point of the heart you've just finished. The exact spacing isn't crucial. Stencil in the same color.
7. Continue to make 2 rows of each color until the fabric is covered with hearts.

Making the bag

1. Turn 1/4 inch of the top raw edge to the wrong side and press.
2. Turn this edge down another 1/2 inch to form a hem. Stitch across hemline.
3. With right sides facing, fold the fabric in half lengthwise. With 1/4-inch seam allowance, stitch down the long raw edge and across the bottom.
4. Clip corners at the bottom and turn right side out.
5. Tie a ribbon tightly around the top seamline of the bag to gather closed.

Gift bag designs

FLOWERPOT

Stencil a group of clay flowerpots, add a plant, and you have a lovely gift. This is a nice touch for a friend in the hospital.

The border design and flowers are stenciled in morning-glory blue. Since each is a one-color design, it's very easy to cut and stencil for a quick, last-minute gift. Consider making these to hold plants for a church bazaar. The added decoration on the pots will cost you very little, you can make several in very little time, and you may add on to the price normally charged.

Materials

Clay flowerpot; tracing paper; pencil; masking tape; stencil paper; X-acto knife; stencil brush; blue and white acrylic paint; dish.

Directions

The clay pot is easy to stencil. The paint is quickly absorbed, the color is a nice background, and no preparation is necessary.

1. Trace the border design. Trace the flower design.
2. Tape a stencil paper over each design on a cutting board and cut out the elements with the craft knife.
3. Cut the strip of border stencil paper so it fits around the lip of the flowerpot. Tape each end of the stencil to the pot.

Stenciling

1. Mix a drop or two of blue paint in the white so it is consistent. Mix enough to complete the job.
2. Dip the stencil brush into the paint, tap the brush up and down a few times on paper, and fill the border area with blue paint. Continue to stencil around the rim, removing and repositioning the stencil as you do so. The last stencil may not be complete if there is only room for a portion of it.
3. Position the flower stencil so it appears to be growing up from the bottom edge. Tape this to the pot.
4. Fill the area with the same blue paint mixture. Remove the stencil and reposition it to the right and then left as you add designs all around. The placement and spacing isn't crucial and can be done by eye.

You can use this stencil in many different colors to create variety even without changing the design. If you are making these for a bazaar sale the decorated pots filled with colorful plants will create a dynamic booth, sure to attract buyers.

Flowerpot

FLOWER BASKET

A basket isn't the easiest surface to stencil on. However, if the basket is a fairly tight, wide, flat weave, it provides a lovely, natural color and texture for a stencil design.

You can stencil a basket for hanging on the door at holiday time, to fill with greens for a table centerpiece, or to hold mail. This design is easy to cut and can be used on many other surfaces.

Materials

Basket; tracing paper; pencil; masking tape; stencil paper; X-acto knife; stencil brushes; red, green, and yellow acrylic paint; saucers or paper plates.

Directions

Since you'll be stenciling right on the basket, no painting or staining is necessary. However, if you want a painted background, apply white latex or acrylic paint with a sponge-type brush for this project. These brushes are inexpensive and found wherever paint is sold.

Cutting the stencils

This is basically a 2-color stencil with a dot of yellow in the center of each flower. You can add this by eye or cut a third stencil for the yellow color.

1. Trace the design and tape a stencil sheet over it on a cutting surface.
2. Cut a stencil for the stem and leaves and another for the flower. If your knife

Flower basket

33

blade is sharp it will be helpful when cutting into tiny areas like this.

3. Make another tracing of the complete flower to use as a positioning guide. Cut the tracing paper to the size of the small section you will stencil on the basket. This will ensure perfect placement of each design.

Stenciling

1. Using the traced flowers as a guide, tape the cutout stencil to a section of the basket.

2. Use a small amount of green paint in a dish and dip your stencil brush into it. Tap off the excess on newspaper.

3. Tap up-and-down through the cutout area to apply paint to the basket. Lift the stencil and move to the next section.

4. Next, position the flower stencil under the tracing guide so it's above the stenciled stem and leaves. Tape to the basket.

5. Apply a small amount of red paint to each flower stencil. Add a yellow circle to the center of each.

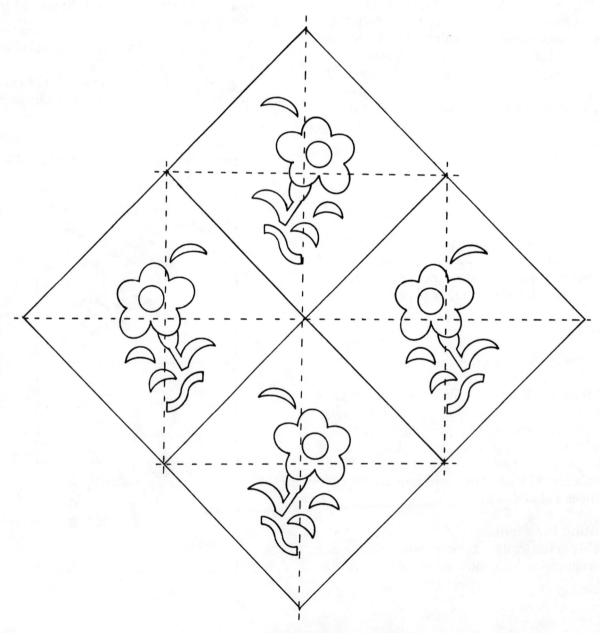

34   *Diagram for stencil placement on basket*

HEART BOXES

A series of graduating heart boxes come as a nesting set and are quite inexpensive, as they are made of thin balsa wood. When stenciled, they make darling gifts as is, but lined with pretty paper and filled with little candies, they're even more terrific.

The stencil designs are appropriately easy to do and are bright and cheerful, filling the top of each. The largest box is 5 × 5 inches, while the smallest is 3 × 3 inches.

Materials

Heart or oval boxes or tins; 1-inch sponge-type paintbrush (found in hardware stores); tracing paper; pencil; masking tape; X-acto knife; stencil paper; blue, green, red, yellow, and white acrylic paint; stencil brushes; paper plates; wrapping paper for lining (optional).

Directions

Using the 1-inch brush, paint the tops, bottoms, and rims of each box in the following colors:

Strawberry: top white, bottom blue
Goose: top blue, bottom red
Morning glory: top white, rim blue, bottom pale green (a drop of green mixed with white)
Palm tree: top blue, rim yellow, bottom green

Cutting the stencils

1. Trace each stencil design. The morning glory is a 2-color stencil. The strawberry has 3 separate stencils: the fruit, the stem, and the seeds. The goose is a 3-color stencil. The palm tree is one stencil and the moon another.
2. Place a piece of stencil paper over each design and tape to a cutting surface. Cut a new stencil for each color. If you stencil all four designs you will have ten different stencils.

Stenciling

Since you have all your colors mixed, you are ready to begin stenciling.

1. *Morning glory:* Position the stem-and-leaf stencil on the large white top. Hold down and fill the area with green paint. Remove the stencil and position the flower stencil.

   To achieve shading so that some areas are darker than others, simply continue to pounce the brush onto the area to be more intense. Do not add more paint to your brush. Remember, it is always best to use an almost dry brush and keep stippling until no more paint comes off the brush. Then add more paint to your brush, tap on newspaper until almost dry, and continue to stencil.

2. *Palm tree:* Center the stencil on the blue box top and stencil with green paint. Re-

Morning glory

Palm tree

move the stencil and position the moon cutout. Stencil this with a minimum of yellow paint on your brush.

3. *Goose:* Place the body stencil on the blue top and apply white paint. This may require another application of paint to completely cover it so the blue doesn't show through the white.

   Next register the feet and bill on the body and stencil with yellow. Last, add the red ribbon to the neck.

4. *Strawberry:* With the red paint, stencil the strawberry to the center of a white top. Position the stem and stencil with green. When this is dry, place the seed stencil over the strawberry and add white paint through the holes until they are opaque.

Finish

You can paint or line the insides with pretty paper. Choose a small print such as that used as wallpaper in dollhouses. This is available through hobby shops. Measure and cut pieces to fit and glue in place. Cut and glue a piece for the bottom to finish the projects.

Additional designs for heart boxes

Additional designs for heart boxes

WELCOME PLAQUE

Resembling the Early American floor cloths, this welcome plaque was created on artist's canvas board. It can be used as a floor mat in an entryway or framed and hung on a wall. The canvas board is 22 × 28 inches and costs approximately $3.00 at an art supply store.

Materials

Artist's canvas; tracing paper; pencil; masking tape; stencil paper; precut stencil letters; X-acto knife; stipple brushes; 2-inch-wide paintbrush; pointed artist's brush; Illinois Bronze Accent acrylic paint colors Wild Honey, Soft White, Ultramarine Blue, Razzle Red.

Directions

Begin by painting the canvas board with Wild Honey. Let the paint dry thoroughly. Since it is acrylic paint, it is easily washed off hands and brush with warm water.

Preparing the design

1. Trace the goose and heart design from the book and tape it to a cutting surface.
2. Tape a sheet of stencil paper over the tracing and, using the X-acto knife, cut out the goose's body.
3. Cut another stencil for the bill, feet, heart, and scarf. Cut this all from one paper as one stencil since the colors do not touch.
4. Trace the checkerboard border design and the star and cut the stencils.

Stenciling

1. Find the center of the plaque and mark where the heart will be stenciled. Do not stencil the heart at this time. You will use this mark to position the geese.
2. Tape the goose body stencil in position on the board and stencil with white paint. Leave the stencil in position and when the paint dries, restencil with a second coat of white in order to cover the background.
3. When the paint is dry again, turn the design over and stencil another goose on the opposite side of the center mark so the geese are facing.
4. Position the second stencil for the bill, feet, and scarf and tape in place. Using black paint, stencil the bill and feet, followed by the scarf and heart in red.
5. Turn the stencil over and finish the second goose in the same way.
6. Using a pointed artist's brush paint a white stripe down the center of each scarf if desired. Add a drop of black paint for each eye.

Welcome plaque stencil

Stenciling letters

1. Trace each letter of the precut stencils on separate pieces of paper.
2. Starting with the letter C in the center, above the heart, tape each letter so it is evenly spaced in an arc.
3. Using the traced letters as a placement guide, stencil each letter with red paint.
4. Stencil a blue star between each letter.

Border

1. Tape the checkerboard stencil approximately 1½ inches down from the top and in from one edge.
2. Using blue paint, stencil 17 squares across for the first line of the border.
3. To make the second line of squares, shift the stencil in order to make a checkerboard and apply blue paint to 16 squares across.

To finish

If this plaque will be used as a floor mat, you might want to spray it with a coating of clear varnish. This will protect the painted finish. To hang, frame it with or without glass.

CHILD'S STEP STOOL

Unfinished furniture items are wonderful for stenciling. Consider the series of small running border designs for a small step stool, a child's chair, dresser drawers, a high chair, or crib.

The acrylic paint made by Illinois Bronze is especially good for stenciling over a painted wooden surface because it is smooth and creamy. There is a wonderful range of colors to choose from. For this step stool I chose their Larkspur Blue and Pink Blossom for the running bunnies.

Materials

Wooden step stool; tracing paper; pencil; stencil paper; stipple brushes; 2-inch-wide paintbrush; masking tape; precut stencil letters; acrylic paints: blue, white, pink; sandpaper; varnish.

Directions

If the wood is rough to the touch, sand it lightly until smooth. Coat all exposed areas with the blue paint and let dry. Sand lightly if necessary and recoat with paint.

Cutting the stencils

1. Trace the bunny designs or design of your choice and arrange them on your stool so you know they will fit the area to be stenciled.
2. Adjust the spacing of the bunnies so the designs fit your object.
3. Tape the stencil paper over the tracing on a cutting surface. Cut out the body of each bunny for the first stencil.
4. Using another piece of stencil paper, cut the tails for the second stencil color.

Stenciling

1. Tape the stencil of the bunny bodies in position and apply pink paint to the object you are stenciling.
2. Let the first 2 stencil bunnies dry, turn the stencil over, and apply the next 2 designs.
3. Continue in this way until you have completed the stencil border.
4. Position the second stencil for the tails and apply white paint. Continue until all bunnies have white tails.
5. Center your precut stencil letters in the center of your object and stencil the name in pink (or color of your choice).

To finish

If you have stenciled a step stool, as I did here, you will want to protect the painted surface with a coat or two of clear varnish.

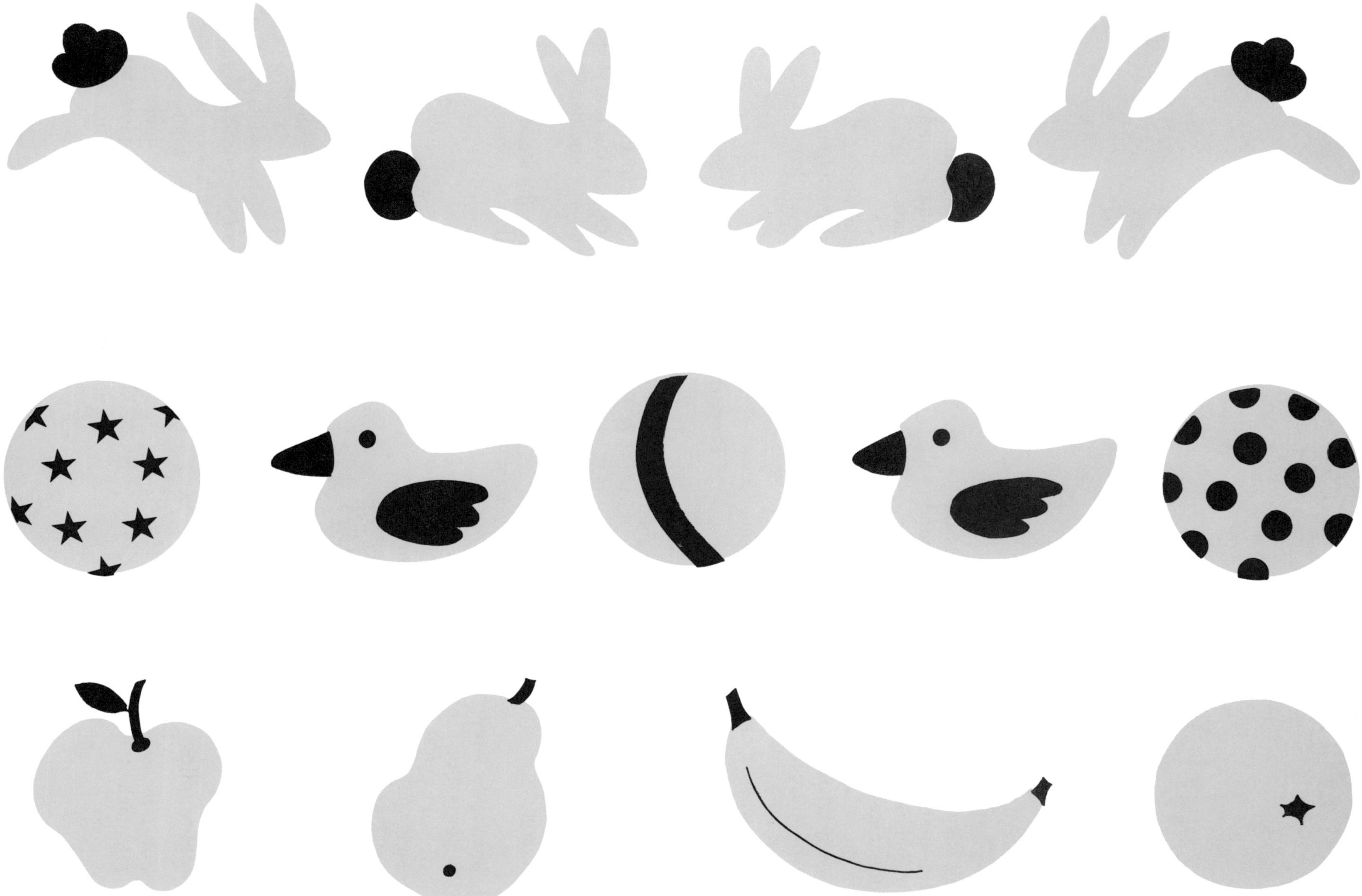

Suggested designs for baby stool

BABY PILLOW

It is as easy to stencil on fabric as it is on wood or other hard surfaces. This is a good way to decorate many fabric items and is especially nice for baby accessories. Use acrylic paint, which is washable but won't wash away when you wash the fabric. There is a line of fabric paints in wonderful country colors that are made by Illinois Bronze. They too can be washed off hands but are permanent on fabric.

The duck design used for the pillow can also be applied to baby's furniture, walls, lampshade, and even clothing. The finished pillow is 11 × 11 inches.

Materials

1/2 yard yellow fabric; 1 1/2 yards red piping; 1 1/2 yards 1-inch eyelet; 1 1/2 yards 2 1/2-inch-wide eyelet ruffle; Polyfil® stuffing; tracing paper; stencil paper; masking tape; X-acto knife; stipple brush; pointed artist's brush; white, orange, and black acrylic paint.

Directions

To prepare pillow

1. Cut 2 pieces of yellow fabric 11 1/2 × 11 1/2 inches.

2. With right sides facing and raw edges aligned, pin the piping around the front of one piece of fabric.
3. Stitch around.
4. Pin the 1-inch eyelet around the edge in this same way and stitch from the wrong side, using the piping stitches as a guide.

Preparing the stencils

1. This is a 2-color stencil. Trace the duck design.
2. Tape the stencil paper over the tracing on a cutting surface. Cut out one stencil for the white body and another for the bill and feet.
3. In order to position the stencils so they are evenly spaced, it is necessary to cut 2 body stencils spaced as they will be on the fabric.

Stenciling

1. Tape the pillow fabric (with the piping and ruffle edge) over newspaper on a hard surface.
2. Measure approximately 1 inch up from the bottom edge of the fabric and run a strip of masking tape across the pillow top. This will give you a straight line above which to place the ducks.
3. Make a tracing of the complete duck to use as a placement guide. Place the trac-

ing above the masking tape line to position the center duck.

4. Slip the body stencil under the tracing so it is in position on the fabric and remove the tracing. Tape the stencil in place and apply the white paint with a stipple brush. Let dry.

5. You may need 2 or more applications of white paint to sufficiently cover the area.

6. Using the stencil as a guide, repeat the ducks to the right and left of the center duck.

7. Tape the second stencil for the feet and bill in position on each duck and apply orange paint.

8. Repeat the line of ducks at the top of the pillow, beginning with a tape line approximately 3¹/2 to 4 inches down from the piping.

To finish

1. With right sides facing and raw edges aligned, pin the 2¹/2-inch-wide ruffled eyelet all around the pillow top.

2. Stitch around.

3. With right sides facing and raw edges aligned, pin the backing fabric to the top of the pillow with the design and edging between.

4. Stitch around 3 sides and 4 corners. Trim fabric all around and clip corners.

5. Turn right side out, stuff with Polyfil®, and slip stitch opening closed.
   Note: For alternative pillow designs, you can use any of the stencils from the "Country Accessories" project that follows.

Duck pillow stencil

COUNTRY ACCESSORIES

The stencil designs provided for the small wooden items can be used in a variety of ways. You can form any pattern with the individual designs and use them in any combination with each other.

The country accessories used here are available in hobby and craft stores or through our mail order source. The small boxes are replicas of early Shaker containers and the wall rack and flower or utility holder are reminiscent of Early American objects. The background color is achieved with Rit dyes, which give the wood a soft, country look. If you choose light colors for the stencils, they will look best.

Materials

A variety of wooden items; tracing paper; pencil; masking tape; stencil paper; X-acto knife; a variety of Rit dye colors (Royal Blue, Fuchsia, Kelly Green, Plum, and Purple were used here); stipple brushes; acrylic paints; varnish, sandpaper, and wax optional.

Directions

If you are stenciling unfinished wooden items, they may need a light sanding if the surface is rough.

1. Dilute about 2 ounces of liquid dye per quart of boiling water. Pour into a container large enough to hold each item. This can be the sink or a pail. Stir the mixture.
2. Immerse the item in the dye solution and remove when the desired color is achieved (less than one minute for most items). Let dry.
3. Determine which designs you will use for each item and how they will be arranged. You can try different arrangements by tracing the designs and placing them on each item.

Cutting the stencils

1. Make a tracing of the area of the object to be stenciled.
2. Trace the stencil designs within this area.
3. With the stencil paper taped over the tracing, cut out each stencil with your X-acto knife.

Stenciling

1. Tape the stencil in position and apply acrylic paint in the colors of your choice. Each of the stencils is designed for one color, which makes them easy to apply.
2. If you are stenciling the goose design with the heart, position the heart in the

Country accessory stencils

center of the area and stencil this first. Next, position the goose stencil first on one side of the heart, then flip it over to stencil another goose on the opposite side.

To finish

1. Once all the stenciled paint has dried, give each item a coat of clear spray varnish. Let dry.

2. Using fine sandpaper, rub over the surface with a light hand.

3. Apply a coat of furniture paste wax. Let dry and rub to a soft shine.

4. You might want to paint the inside of the boxes or line them with pretty paper. An overall small print often found on wrapping paper or dollhouse wallpaper is perfect for this.

5. To protect the paper lining, coat with varnish.

PLATE 14   *Flowering Table*

PLATE 15   *Pineapple Table*

PLATE 16   *Kitchen Stools*

PLATE 17 Bed Headboard, Footstool, Night Table Cabinet

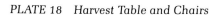

PLATE 18 Harvest Table and Chairs

PLATE 19 Desk Corner, Mirror Frame, Curtains, Wall Stencil

Book Three

First Steps in Stenciling on Furniture

A stencil design can be adapted for different furniture pieces and can be applied over a painted, stained, or glazed background. When a surface is very shiny, or has a glossy finish, the stencil doesn't adhere very well.

Stenciling is a good way to dress up an old piece of furniture, but it's important to remove any oil or wax and to sand the surface.

I've found that unfinished furniture is perfect for most stencil projects. The raw wood can be painted with a flat latex in any color or it can be stained. Oil base stains such as Min-Wax are sold in paint stores and you can see samples which show you how various colors will look on your wood.

The following projects utilize typical pieces that are easy to find, or ones that you are likely to own. They are fairly standard in size and use, and the designs are, therefore, applicable for most pieces.

The drop-leaf dining table has a stained background while the chairs are painted with a flat latex. The headboard of the bed is also stained and the stencil design is repeated on the decorative pillow.

Ordinary kitchen stools will hardly look everyday when you paint them in contrasting pastels and add stenciled border designs to each.

The round dining table illustrates the way you can use your china pattern or fabric print to create a matching stencil. This project will demonstrate the way to do this with any design.

Preparing furniture for stencil

If you are starting with raw wood, the piece should be completely sanded. Apply a coat of shellac or primer paint to seal the pores. When dry, sand lightly again and wipe away the sanding dust. The furniture is now ready to be painted or stained.

If your furniture has a finish, remove the wax by washing it with turpentine or denatured alcohol. If you're starting with a painted surface, you may be able to stencil right over it, but you may wish to repaint the background first.

When a piece of furniture is painted, it may require 3 or 4 coats to sufficiently cover it. Choose a background color a shade or two lighter than the paper sample in the paint store. When a large area is saturated with color, it often looks darker or more intense than it does on a small swatch.

I have chosen country colors for these pieces. They create an interesting subdued background to enhance the stencils. Ivory color, as used on the round table, is also especially pleasing.

After the furniture has been given a final coat of paint, it should be lightly sanded for a smooth finish. Each piece has a coat of flat varnish over all for added protection.

FLOWERING TABLE

This design was created to fit on a round table. The origin was a border on a salad plate found in a thrift shop.

Often chinaware is an excellent source for such designs, which, once enlarged, serve as decoration on a larger scale. The tabletop used for this is six times larger than the plate. For the directions to enlarge any design, refer to pages x–xi.

Stenciled in bright pink with green leaves, the flower border looks best on an ivory-colored background. However, you can use any color combination to match your decor. When stenciling furniture, plan where the item will be used in order to select the colors. This is not just an accessory or room accent, but a fairly prominent statement.

Materials

Medium-grade sandpaper; semi-gloss antique white latex paint; 2½-inch all-purpose paintbrush; tracing paper; pencil; masking tape; stencil paper; X-acto knife; stencil brushes; pink, white, and green acrylic paints; saucers; pint of satin finish varnish; brush cleaner; fine sandpaper or steel wool; clear furniture paste wax; soft rag.

Directions

If necessary, remove the old finish on the table. If the table isn't in bad shape, simply sand the surface and give it a coat of latex paint. When dry, add a second coat.

1. Tape pieces of tracing paper together to create a large-enough piece to cover your tabletop.
2. Trace the border design in position inside the tabletop outline. Continue to retrace it to be sure it will fit all around.
3. Adjust the size by eliminating or expanding the elements. If it is too large, remove a small leaf from the design. If it's too small, add a leaf, or leave more space between the sections. This tracing will be your placement guide.

Cutting the stencil

1. Tape the stencil to the tracing of the border section and place on a cutting surface.
2. Use your X-acto knife to cut each stencil. Tendrils, leaves, stems, and flower petals are cut from one stencil sheet.
3. All but the flower petals are green. Mask out the petal areas where they touch or meet the green stems and flower base.

Mixing the paint

The colors used for this are pastel pink and green and may require mixing if the paints straight from the tube are too bright.

Take care to mix enough of each color at one time to finish the job. Use a large amount of white while adding a drop of color at a time to achieve the desired shade. A palette knife or other flat utensil should be used to mix and blend the paints until the color is consistent. A damp paper towel placed over each mixing dish will keep the paints from drying out.

Stenciling

1. Position the cutout stencil sheet on the tabletop according to the layout diagram and secure it with masking tape so that it doesn't slip while stenciling.
2. Begin with the green areas and dip the stipple brush into the paint. Tap up-and-down on newspaper to remove excess paint and stencil with a minimum amount on your brush. Let the paint dry and, before removing the stencil, reapply paint in the same way if needed.

   Continue to apply one color all the way around before moving on to the next color. Save a small amount of each color paint for touch-ups.
3. Remove masking tape from the petal areas and mask out the stems on both sides of the petals. Mask out the flower base. This prevents pink paint from getting on the green areas.
4. Apply pink paint all around to complete the design.

Finish

To protect the surface and make it glow, varnish the entire piece with the satin varnish. Begin at the center of the tabletop and draw your brush to the outer edges, working across the surface.

When the varnish is completely dry, sand the surface very lightly or rub over it with fine steel wool. Coat the table with clear paste wax and buff it to a shine with a soft rag.

6

Placement diagram for flowering table

PINEAPPLE TABLE

A pineapple stencil will fit on the top of almost any size table. Add a delicately curved border all around and you'll have a table reminiscent of traditional American design.

This table is fairly common—you may even have a similar one. If it needs a coat of paint, you can easily sand and repaint it for your stencil background.

Materials

Sandpaper; light-ocher-color latex paint; 2-inch-wide paintbrush; tracing paper; pencil; masking tape; stencil paper; X-acto knife; stencil brushes; burnt orange and green acrylic paint; saucers or paper plates.

Directions

Begin by preparing the furniture piece. Sand the wood and give it a coat of paint. The background color used here is light ocher or a mustard yellow. Apply the number of coats needed for a smooth, opaque surface.

Preparing the stencils

1. With tracing paper over the tabletop, draw the outline of the table.
2. Trace the stencils of the pineapple body and leaves in the center of the outline.

3. Trace the border elements provided here to make up one quarter of the outline.
4. Lift the tracing, flip it over, and trace the design on the opposite side so the border design joins and is continuous. Adjust the design if it doesn't fit perfectly. Since all tables are not exactly the same size, you'll need to adapt the design to fit the area. Tape the entire tracing on the top of the table at 2 points just to hold it conveniently as a placement guide for your stencils.

Cutting the stencils

1. Trace the stencils. Tape stencil paper to the traced design and place on a cutting surface.
2. Using a craft knife, cut out each section of the design. The blade should be clean and sharp to achieve even strokes for nice fluid curves.
3. With your tracing as a guide, slide the stencil beneath the paper and tape the body of the pineapple to the center of the table. Lift the tracing out of the way temporarily.

Stenciling

To achieve the burnt orange hue for the pineapple and border it may be necessary to mix it yourself. I used equal amounts of Grumbacher's Cadmium Orange and a color called Portrayt.

Always use a dry brush to stencil. If the paint is runny, it will surely seep under a stencil such as this where the cutout areas are separated only by narrow uncut sections.

1. With a small amount of paint in a saucer, stencil the pineapple body.

    Try to stencil from the outside of the design inward. Move from one area to another as the paint fills in the openings. Do not overload each area with paint. A small amount covers quite a bit of space. If an area hasn't been sufficiently covered, you can go over it again after it is dry in the same way.

2. When the body of the pineapple is complete, remove the stencil and, using your tracing guide, position the leaves. Tap the green paint onto the stencil as before. Using a straight-up-and-down motion, tap a tiny bit of color onto the surface. Continue to do this until the leaf cutouts are filled in.

3. When all cut-away areas have been filled in with color and the paint is dry, peel the stencil sheet away from the tabletop. Your design should be perfect. You can now go on to the border design.

Border

Since this is a delicate stencil, you'll need to take a bit more care when applying the paint.

1. Tape the section of the border in position using your tracing as a guide.

2. Tap the burnt orange paint onto the stencil.

3. Carefully lift the design and reposition it, moving along in this way as you do each section.
    Note: To avoid smudging, be sure the paint is dry in each section before placing the stencil sheet down again. Acrylic paint dries quickly.

4. Follow the diagram and add the green leaves where indicated all around the border. This will add color and interest to the border and tie in with the center design.

Finish

To protect the design from wearing with use, you can give the entire table a coat of semi-gloss wood varnish. Polyurethane is excellent for this.

Apply the varnish in long strokes, beginning in the center of the table and working out to the edges. A thin coat is best. The varnish will take twenty-four hours to dry. Once dry, a second coat is recommended.

Lightly rub over the entire piece with some very fine steel wool. Give the table a coat of clear paste wax, buff with a soft rag, and you're finished.

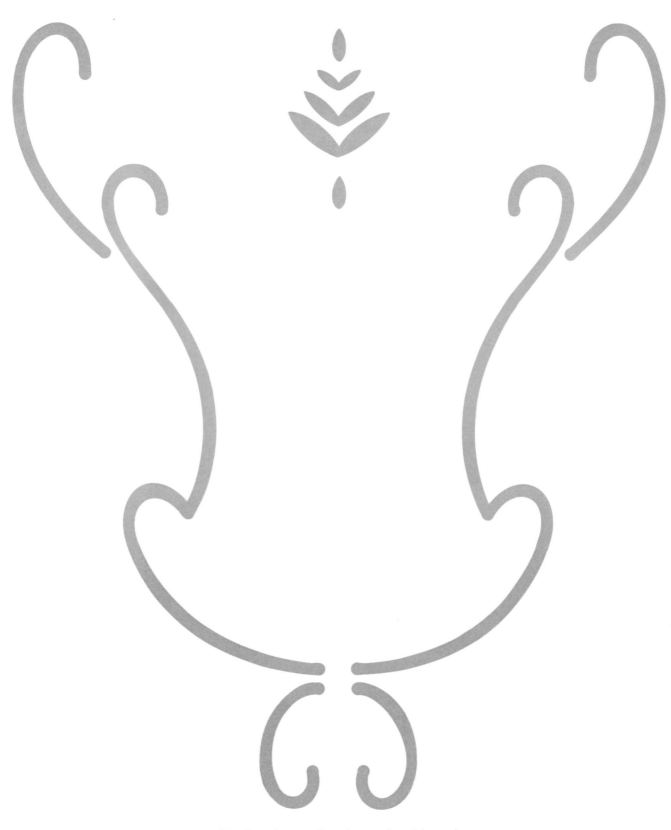

Border element for pineapple table

Pineapple table—body and leaves stencils

KITCHEN STOOLS

Round wooden kitchen stools are fairly common and come in different heights. They are inexpensive and provide the perfect shape and surface on top for a design. Notice these two stools use the same design, but in reverse. This is an example of how a little imagination can take your stenciling into all sorts of directions. The legs of each are painted with a darker shade of the stencil color.

Materials

Wooden stools; sandpaper (medium weight); Shaker blue, barn-red, and white latex paints; 2-inch paintbrush; tracing paper; pencil; masking tape; stencil paper; X-acto knife; stencil brushes; saucers or paper plates.

Directions

Lightly sand the stools. Paint the base of one with the Shaker blue color, the other with barn-red paint. Let dry and paint again.

Apply 2 or 3 coats of white paint to the top of the stool with the blue base. Sand lightly and paint again if needed.

Mix a drop of the red paint into a saucer of white and mix to achieve a pastel pink. Apply 2 or 3 coats of paint to the top of the stool with the red base.

Preparing the stencils

1. Using a piece of tracing paper large enough to cover the stool top, trace the lines on the diagram of each stool from the book following the placement layout for each design.
2. Place the tracing on the center of each stool and extend the drawn lines to the edge of the stool.
3. Make a tracing of each of the 3 stencils to be cut out.

Cutting the stencils

1. Tape stencil paper over the traced design and place on a cutting surface.
2. Using the craft knife, cut out each stencil. A paper punch is handy for cutting perfect circles.

Stenciling

Latex paint is thinner than acrylic paint. This requires more care when stenciling so that paint doesn't seep under the stencil edges. Be sure to tap excess paint onto newspaper so that your brush is almost dry before beginning.

Stool A

1. Tape the tracing with the drawn lines at 2 points (as shown on diagram) on the white stool top.

Kitchen stool stencil elements

2. Slide the border stencil for stool A under the tracing and position it on one line as indicated.
3. Lift the tracing and stipple the blue paint with an almost-dry brush.
4. Continue to move the stencil around to create the border.
5. Use the tracing as a guide to position the inner circle design. Plan to have the flower stems meet in the center. (See diagram.)

Stool B

1. With the tracing guide taped to the top of the stool (pink top), slide the flower stencils under the tracing to position on either side of the drawn lines.

2. Remove the tracing paper and tape the stencil, or hold firmly on the stool top while you stipple each element with blue paint.
3. Use the lines on the tracing as a positioning guide for arranging the inner border.
4. Remove the tracing once again, hold the stencil in place, and stencil the inner border with the barn-red paint.

Finish

When the paint is dry, give the entire stool a coat of flat matte varnish. Let this dry and reapply. This is an optional step that will protect the paint finish.

Placement diagram for kitchen stool A

Placement diagram for kitchen stool B

BED HEADBOARD

The back of a bed is a good area for applying a stencil design. A one-color stencil is especially pretty on a painted or stained background. If you keep it simple and confine the design to a border area along the top of a headboard, it will be visible even when pillows are propped up against it. Use the same design in a contrasting color on fabric to make accent pillows to match.

Materials

Wooden surface; tracing paper; pencil; masking tape; stencil paper; X-acto knife; white acrylic paint (if background is stained or a dark painted color); stencil brush; saucer.

Directions

This is a one-color stencil that can be used in numerous ways. It creates a running border on the headboard and an overall, evenly spaced pattern on the pillow.

1. Trace the design and tape it over white paper on a cutting surface. Tape the stencil over this.
2. Using the X-acto knife, cut out the stencil.

3. Remove the stencil sheet and save the white paper to trace more designs if needed later.

Stenciling the headboard

1. Position the stencil on the edge of one end of the headboard.
2. Trim the excess paper that extends beyond the top of the edge of the bed and tape the stencil to the surface.
3. Squirt a small amount of paint in a saucer. Since you won't be mixing paint, you can add more as often as needed. Dip the stencil brush into the paint and tap off excess on newspaper.
4. Because you are stenciling from an awkward angle, find a comfortable position for applying the paint. Keep the brush especially dry since you are applying the paint to a vertical object.

Bed headboard stencil

5. Lift the stencil and move it forward with a small amount of space between each design. Tape it in position and continue to apply the paint.

Your pillow can be 12 or 14 inches square, which are the standard-size forms sold in five-and-dime or notions stores.

Extra materials

1/2 yard muslin; 1 1/2 yards piping (color of your choice) for a 12-inch pillow, 58 inches for a 14-inch pillow; pillow form to size; green acrylic paint.

Directions

1. Draw a 12 1/2- or 14 1/2-inch square on muslin.
2. Cut out 2 pieces and set backing piece aside.
3. Tape the muslin square at each corner so it is taut on a piece of cardboard. Place this on a cutting surface.
4. Tape the cut stencil from the headboard in position at the upper-left-hand corner of the square. Leave approximately one inch all around from drawn edges.

5. Using green paint, stipple through the stencil onto the fabric. Remove and repeat on the opposite corner.
6. Position the stencil equidistant between the corner stencils and apply the paint.
7. When stenciling the next row down, position the stencils under the space between the stencils above. The second row will have only 2 designs. For the third row, repeat row one.

Estimate the placement of each stencil by eye. When stenciling on fabric that will be made into a pillow cover, the shape and curving over the pillow form compensates for imperfect spacing that would be more apparent on a flat surface.

Making the pillow

Once the fabric has been stenciled, remove it from the cardboard.

1. With raw edges even with the drawn pencil line, pin the piping to the pillow front all around. Overlap the ends where they meet.
2. Using a zipper foot, stitch all around with 1/4-inch seam allowance.
3. Place the muslin backing over the stenciled top and pin together.
4. Using the stitch line of the piping as a guide, sew around 3 sides and 4 corners. Clip corners and turn right side out.
5. Stuff with a pillow form and slip stitch the opening closed.

Border layout for headboard

FOOTSTOOL

A small, wooden, two-step stool is handy for out-of-reach items on a closet shelf. Stencil a pretty ribbon design as a 2-color repeat pattern in pastels over a dark background. This will be a nice accent piece in your bedroom.

Since this is a repeat border design, it has many uses. You can use it on dresser drawers or as a frame for a window. Use two or three of the rows as a window shade or curtain border. And it would be especially pretty across the hemline of a top sheet or pillowcase.

Materials

Object to be stenciled; tracing paper; pencil; stencil sheet; X-acto knife; forest green latex paint; 2-inch paintbrush; red, blue, and white acrylic paint; stencil brushes; saucers or paper plates; varnish; brush cleaner.

Directions

If you are using a raw piece of furniture, it may need to be sanded before painting. If so, use a medium-grade sandpaper for this.

When using a dark-color paint such as this forest green, one coat should cover sufficiently. If you paint the background with a light color, you may need 2 or 3 coats.

Cutting the stencils

Since this is a 2-color design, you will cut 2 separate stencils.

1. Trace stencil A for the blue half-moon and 2 dots. Trace stencil B for the pink half-moon and dots.
2. Tape a piece of stencil paper over each tracing and place on a cutting surface.
3. Using the X-acto knife, cut out each stencil. A paper punch is helpful for making perfect circles if you can get it into the correct position.

Stenciling

Before applying the paint, you have to plan the design so your patterns will be in a perfectly straight line. Keep in mind that since all objects are not the same size, you may have to adjust the design slightly to fit your surface.

1. Begin by drawing the outline of the step stool on tracing paper.
2. Divide the area into evenly spaced lengthwise segments using the stencil pattern to determine the distance between each. This will be your placement guide.
3. Begin at the lower left. Lift the tracing slightly and tape the first stencil of a half-moon and 2 dots in position on the drawn line, as indicated on your tracing.

Lift tracing out of the way temporarily.

4. Mix a drop of blue paint with a table-spoonful of white to create a pale pastel color.
5. Dip your brush into the paint, tap up and down a few times on newspaper, and stencil onto the stool.
6. Continue across with the blue paint, using the stencil itself to register each successive area. As you reposition the half-moon and dots, the cutout to the left will always cover the previously stenciled dot.
7. Repeat the blue stencil (A) across the stool on each pencil line of the tracing paper guide.
8. Using a clean dry brush, stencil the second stencil (B) with pale pink paint (mixed as for the blue).

Since there are a lot of elements here, you will always have a point of register to keep the design on course.

Finish

A step stool gets a lot of use that can wear away the design. To protect the paint, I would recommend a coat or two of varnish. You can use a high-gloss varnish for a shiny finish or a satin varnish for a matte finish. It will take 24 hours to dry.

Step stool stencil

NIGHT TABLE CABINET

This is a reproduction of an Early American cupboard with a drawer and covered shelf area. It is available from manufacturers of unfinished furniture and is a typical size. Therefore, if you can't find this particular item, you may have something similar that would look equally well with this stencil decoration.

The designs incorporate part of the border used on the desk, kitchen stools, and bedside footstool. The background color is burnt orange and the stencil is dark green.

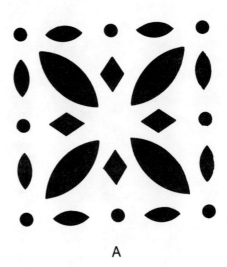

A

Materials

Wooden object; burnt orange latex paint; medium-grade sandpaper; 2-inch-wide paintbrush; tracing paper; pencil; masking tape; stencil paper; X-acto knife; green acrylic paint; saucer; varnish; brush cleaner.

Directions

Prepare the wood background for stenciling. If it is raw wood, sand it smooth before applying paint. You will need at least 2 coats to cover sufficiently.

C

Cutting the stencils

1. Trace stencils A, B, C, D, and E on tracing paper.
2. Tape a piece of stencil paper over the tracing of stencil A and place on a cutting surface. Cut this out and set aside.
3. Repeat with stencils B, C, D, and E.

Stenciling

Refer to the stencil placement diagram and the night table cabinet photograph for positioning of your stencils.

1. Remove the drawer and tape stencil A to the center of the drawer front.
2. Squirt a small puddle of green paint into a saucer and dip your brush into it. Tap up and down on newspaper. Apply

B

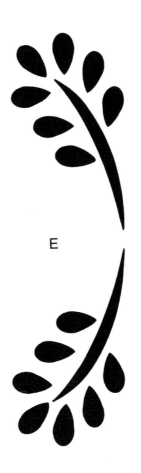

E

D

Night table cabinet stencils

paint with a firm up-and-down motion onto the stencil area. Let dry.

3. Remove the stencil and reposition it to the left of the one just finished, using the corner dot to register the stencil. (See stencil placement diagram.)
4. Stencil as before and repeat the process once more to the left of this stencil.
5. Reposition the stencil to the right of the center design on the drawer front.
6. Stencil as before and repeat the process once more to the right of the design just stenciled.

Stenciling the door

1. Stencil each corner of the door with stencil C in the same manner as you stenciled with A.
2. Position the ribbon border B between the corner elements and add the color.
3. Use the D stencil to create the pattern for the door panel. The corners on the center panel are the inside elements from C. Stencil A appears in the middle of the door.

Finish

To protect the furniture and give your piece a nice luster, apply a coat or two of satin varnish.

Do not overload your brush. Stroke the varnish on lightly in one direction so that it thins as you reach the edges. This will prevent any drip marks. Let dry overnight.

Placement diagram of elements for night table cabinet (Corner dot is the register element for stencil A)

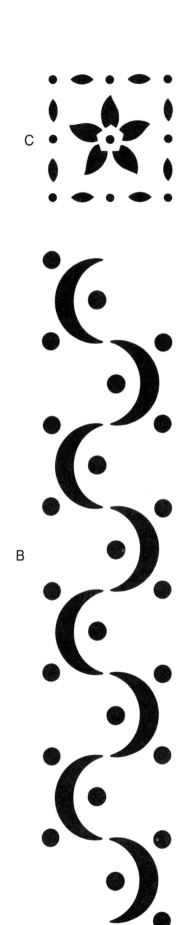

HARVEST TABLE AND CHAIRS

Wood stain creates an interesting background for a colorful as well as subtle design. Only raw wood should be stained.

This pretty harvest table is a common one often found in furniture stores that sell unfinished pieces. The stain brings out the wood grain, and you'd never know it was an inexpensive table underneath. A good oil-base stain will penetrate into the wood and seal it.

A border can be created with individual repeat patterns. This grape design is used on the chair as a single one-color stencil, while is appears in repeat as a 2-color stencil on the table border.

Materials

For the table: wood stain; 3-inch-wide sponge-type brush (available in paint or hardware stores); dry rag; tracing paper; pencil; masking tape; stencil paper; X-acto knife; stencil brushes; green, purple, and white acrylic paints; saucers or paper plates.

For the chairs: Wine-colored latex paint; 2-inch-wide paintbrush; pint of varnish; brush cleaner.

Directions

Prepare the table according to the directions on the wood stain. Paint the chairs in the desired color.

Preparing the stencils

1. Trace the design on a strip of paper as long as your table.
2. Plan the border so each grouping of leaves and grapes is evenly spaced all around. Adjust the spacing to accommodate the table dimensions.
3. Cut the strip of tracing paper so the design is approximately 1½ inches from the bottom edge. Use this as a guide for applying stencils in position.

Cutting the stencils

1. Trace one grouping of the design. Tape the stencil paper over this. When cutting, be sure to leave a generous margin all around on the paper.
2. Using a craft knife, cut out the leaves and stems. This is a delicate area and requires a sharp blade.
3. Cut the grape cluster design. Use a paper punch, if you can, for the grapes. If it won't get far enough into position, cut circles with the knife.
4. Slide the leaf stencil under the tracing in position on the table. Trim the bottom portion of the stencil paper so it is flush against the table like the tracing paper.

Stenciling

1. Tape the stem-and-leaf design onto the tabletop and remove the guide.
2. Squirt a generous amount of green paint

Harvest table stencil

into a saucer and dip the stencil brush into the paint.

3. Tap the brush onto newspaper to remove excess paint and stipple onto the cutout area.

4. Lift the stencil and reposition it under the tracing paper guide once again. Remove tracing and continue to stencil the border.

5. Tape the grape cluster stencil in position between the leaves. Use the tracing to be sure you have placed it accurately.

6. Add a drop of white paint to a puddle of purple paint in a saucer to mix the lavender color.

7. Stencil as for the leaves all around.

8. Rinse both stencils (if acetate) in warm water to clean them. If your stencil is waxed paper, sponge it off carefully and let dry. Rinse the stencil brush and let dry thoroughly. This is done when you will use the same stencil again with a different color paint, or if you have used it extensively over and over again.

Stenciling the chairs

1. Find the center of each chairback.

2. Tape the stem-and-leaf stencil in place and hold it flush against the surface while stenciling. Some chairbacks curve

slightly and it's difficult to tape the stencil flat, but it's important to hold it there while applying the paint.

3. Lean the chairback against something sturdy and apply white paint with a firm, pouncing motion.

   Because you are adding white paint over a dark color, you may have to apply the paint 2 or 3 times.

4. Repeat with the grape cluster stencil in place.

Finish

If you want to give each piece of furniture a coat of varnish, this will protect the paint and give it a lustrous finish. If you do this, let it dry thoroughly overnight.

A COUNTRY STUDY

This is a good example of how you can use a stencil to coordinate several elements in the room. One very simple border design is used many ways on different backgrounds: the desk, curtains, mirror frame, and wall.

Materials

Objects to be stenciled; light green latex paint; paintbrush; muslin for curtains; tracing paper; masking tape; pencil; stencil paper; X-acto craft knife; stencil brushes; dark green, yellow, and red acrylic paints; paper plates.

Directions

The desk used for this project is an unfinished piece of furniture; however, you can adapt this design to fit any furniture with straight lines. The mirror frame is a perfect background for a border and you can adjust this design to fit any flat frame.

Begin by painting or staining the wood objects. Latex paint is best for large projects, as acrylic paint is more costly. If the wood is rough, you should sand it first, then apply a primer coat of paint before the final color. If you use wood stain, follow directions on the can.

Tips for making borders fit the objects

1. Measure all dimensions. For example, on the desk, make sure the border fits *both* vertically and horizontally. To do this, make a tracing of the stencil and lay it out in position on the surface.
2. If the stencil stops in the middle of one square unit it will look fine. Fitting is a problem when the design hits the edge of the surface somewhere between the middle and end of a square unit. In this case, either end the design at the midpoint of a unit, or space the elements a tiny bit further apart to allow for this.
3. The mirror frame has borders on each of the four sides. Because of its design, there are no corners on the frame. For a similar frame *with* corners, a separate design motif can be placed in the corner position. This is used as an accent or to help make a perfect fit. An alternative method is to continue the border all the way around, as was done for the table.

Fitting a border to an edge

A border must fit horizontally and vertically on the surface as well as parallel to the edge and equidistant all around. The easiest way to do this is to measure and cut the edge of the stencil sheet to fit without overlap. For example, if the border is to be 1/2 inch from the edge, cut the stencil paper exactly 1/2 inch

Stenciling on a diagonal

from the bottom of the design. Tape this to the edge of the surface when stenciling. In this way, wherever you attach the stencil it will appear with a 1/2-inch border.

Stenciling on a diagonal

For the wall stencil, you will have to work on the diagonal. This is best done with the aid of a 45° plastic triangle (available in art supply stores). Using the wall stencil behind the desk as an example, measure out the desired distance you want between border stencils. For example, you might make pencil marks every 2 inches, or for this exact project the spacing should be approximately 4 inches apart so there will be 2 inches between each stenciled border. Each complete design is 2 inches wide.

With the short edge of the triangle riding along the baseboard or floor, to ensure a consistent angle, draw a very light pencil line along the long triangle edge from one point to the other. Move the triangle to the next spacing and continue. When stenciling, you will use these lines as the guide for placement of the designs. If you are planning to stencil an entire wall, simply extend the predrawn lines with a yardstick.

Desk

1. Trace the border design and tape a piece of stencil paper on top. Cut a stencil for each color. There are 3 colors.

2. Make a tracing of the border as it will appear on the desk. Tape this at each end on the desk to use as a placement guide.

3. Beginning with stencil A, which is the center of the design, slip it under the tracing and tape in position at one corner of the desktop. Lift the tracing.

4. Using the yellow paint, dip your brush into it and then tap off the excess onto newspaper. Tap up and down over the cutout area of the stencil, taking care not to get paint on the surface of the desk. When dry, lift the stencil and reposition it according to the tracing guide. Continue to fill in color all around the complete border.

   As you can see from the photograph, the full stencil design is used only on the front and sides of the desktop. The design is simplified for the very top area. Use a clean dry brush for each new color.

5. Next position stencil B under the tracing, lift the guide, and stencil all the way around with dark green paint. Using red paint, continue with stencil C, which is repeated on the very top section of the desk.

6. Add a dot of dark green paint to the center of each design on the very top border of the desk only.

Desk and curtain stencil

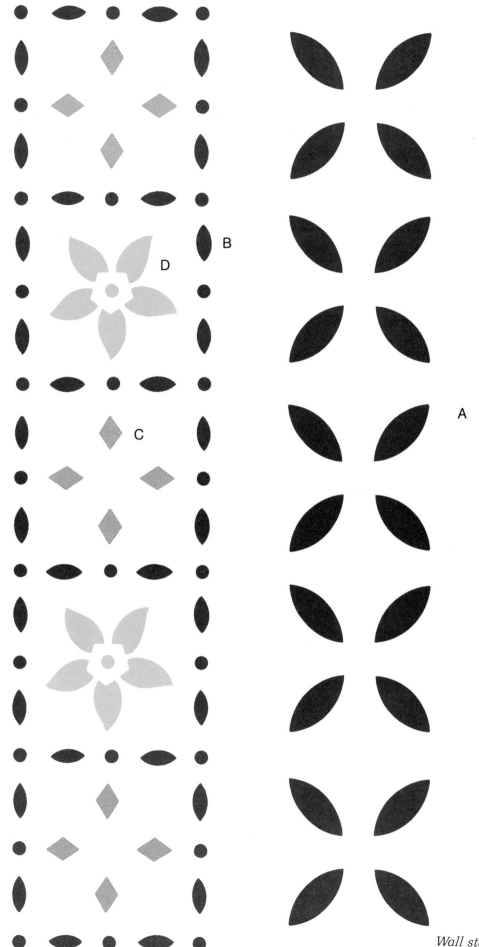

Mirror frame stencil

B

D

A

C

Wall stencil

Curtains

Unbleached muslin is often used for a stenciled background. It receives the paint well and has a country look that goes well with most stencil patterns. The curtains take the full stencil design, which is done in one color. This makes them look slightly different from the others done in 2 or more colors. If you like this look, you might consider doing all the stencils in one color, in which case you can cut one border stencil rather than a different one for each color.

Plan the placement and spacing in the same way as for the desk and mirror. Trace the full design and cut out as one stencil. Tape the fabric to a padded, hard surface so it is taut.

Use a tracing guide for placement and apply dark green paint with an almost-dry brush through the stencil cutout.

Remember, mistakes are permanent on fabric, so make some tests on paper before you start.

Mirror frame

1. Make a tracing of the design to fit the frame.
2. Use the tracing to adjust the spacing of the design elements.

3. Tape the tracing to the frame at each top corner of the paper. Slide stencil B under the tracing paper and tape in position. Lift the tracing out of the way temporarily.
4. Apply paint as before to the cutout areas of the stencil all around the border.
5. Continue to use the tracing as a guide for placing stencils C and D in position.

Wall stencil

Plan the layout on paper to allow for pleasing spacing. This design is greatly simplified since only one element of the stencil is used. The inside panel is painted ivory with stencil A done in dark green. The border around the panel is painted blue, with stencil A done with ivory-colored paint. Since everyone's wall areas are different, you will have to plan the design accordingly. However, this is such a simple border that it will fit wherever you apply it. Refer to the beginning of the "Country Study" projects for specific tips.

A tracing of the entire area to be stenciled will give you a guide to follow as with the mirror frame and desk. Start in the center of each line and work outward, alternating on the right and left to each side of the center design. In this way, the previously stenciled area can dry while you complete another section far enough away to avoid smudging.